Startup CRO

A Field Guide to Scaling up Your Company's Sales Function

Matt Blumberg and Anita Absey

Bolster Network

Contents

Foreword

Scott Dorsey

As a first-time tech founder and CEO at ExactTarget, one phrase kept ringing through my head: "I don't know what I don't know." Even with 10+ years of business experience and a freshly minted MBA degree, I had so many blind spots having never built software, raised venture capital or even led a multi-functional organization. Filling in these gaps took many years and lots of trial and error.

One of my gap-filling strategies was to learn from other CEOs going through similar highs and lows of scaling their company. On this journey, I was fortunate to meet Matt Blumberg. As CEO of Return Path, Matt was building a high growth company in the same digital marketing industry as me. I was impressed by his leadership, strategic thinking, and commitment to helping other entrepreneurs. We became fast friends and we both looked forward to learning from one another.

Matt was always gracious and willing to take my call or have dinner together. Our conversations covered every topic imaginable from leadership to board management to strategic partnerships to international expansion. My advice to entrepreneurs and leaders––build your peer network and spend time developing and nurturing these relationships. While board members and advisors are an important source of knowledge, learning from peers can be invaluable.

One of the highlights of my relationship with Matt was when we were both invited to the White House to witness President Obama signing the Jumpstart our Business Startups Act (or JOBS Act) in April of 2012. With bi-partisan support, the law opened up crowdfunding for startups and streamlined the IPO path. ExactTarget had just gone public two weeks prior so I knew the benefits that the JOBS Act would bring to entrepreneurs. But what I didn't know in April 2012 was that the event would foreshadow my relationship with Matt and how we would work together supporting entrepreneurs and startup ecosystems.

Fast forward to 2020. We are facing unprecedented challenges in the world and the need for innovation and leadership has never been greater. CEOs and functional leaders need tools and resources to accelerate their learning curves and the learning curves of those around them. Speed of learning, thought, and action are more important now than ever. This is why I am so excited about Matt's latest book, *Startup CXO*.

Startup CXO provides a comprehensive field guide to starting and scaling tech companies. Really, the information is super helpful to any company. It provides a "book within a book" framework to enable and empower readers to jump into any section as needed. And it's written by practitioners who provide tons of tangible advice and actionable insights. By reading this book, I believe that leaders will be better equipped to build great companies and anticipate what's around every corner.

In my view, the best CEOs have a grasp of all functions. They can go a mile wide and a couple inches deep. They hire A+ talent and build a culture that brings out the very best in people. They understand how Sales and Marketing fit together, they value HR, Finance, and Legal and understand their interdependencies, they have a clear vision for how Product and Engineering fit together, they know how to be aggressive and how to manage risk, and so much more.

So, *Startup CXO* is an amazing resource for CEOs but also for functional leaders and professionals at any stage of their career. The best functional leaders and professionals understand that cross-functional teamwork is everything. It's so important to have insight and empathy for how other areas of the organization operate. The big picture is needed to see how all of the puzzle pieces fit together.

I feel so lucky that through our venture studio, High Alpha, I have the opportunity to work with Matt and his leadership team as we build

Bolster––a talent marketplace for startup and scaleup tech companies. We are living and applying the concepts and lessons contained in this very book!

My wish for you is that reading *Startup CXO* minimizes your "I don't know what I don't know" list; that it accelerates your development, your curiosity, your ability to ask the right questions, and helps you surround yourself with the right talent. My wish is that you dream big, lead with purpose and integrity, and master your craft. I hope—and believe—that *Startup CXO* will be a helpful companion for you on your company-building journey.

Good luck!

Scott Dorsey

Managing Partner – High Alpha

November 2020

Update for 2024 Edition

I was delighted to hear that Matt and his leadership team at Bolster are breaking out *Startup CXO* into a series of enhanced mini-books to cover the "big 5" functions in a startup -- Finance, HR, Sales, Marketing, and Product/Tech. Each of these mini books provides the reader with a streamlined view of the critical elements of a single leadership function in a startup and highlights some of the best thinking around how to hire and lead teams. This book is power-packed with actionable insights that will serve as a valuable resource as startup teams scale.

Enjoy!

Scott Dorsey

Managing Partner – High Alpha

August 2024

Introduction

Matt Blumberg

In 2020 we sold Return Path, a company we had grown from a startup to over 500 employees over two decades. I documented the CEO journey in *Startup CEO: A Field Guide to Scaling Up Your Business,* but after publishing Startup CEO I was left with the nagging feeling that it wasn't enough to only help CEOs excel, because starting and scaling a business is a collective effort. What about the other critical leadership functions that are needed to grow a company? If you're leading HR, or Finance, or Marketing, or any key function inside a startup, what resources are available to you? What should you be thinking about? What does "great" look like for your function? What challenges lurk around the corner as you scale your function that you might not be focused on today? What are your fellow executives focused on in their own departments, and how can you best work together? If you're a CEO who has never managed all these functions before, what should you be looking for when you hire and manage all these people? If you're an aspiring executive, from entry-level to manager to director, what do you need to think about as you grow your career and develop your skills? And if you're a Board client or investor, what scorecard or metrics are you using to ensure your companies and investments are achieving greatness?

A number of my Return Path colleagues and I founded Bolster shortly after exiting Return Path and we started thinking about a new book as a sequel or companion to *Startup CEO*. That was the origin of *Startup CXO: A Field Guide to Scaling Up Your Company's Critical Functions and Teams. Startup CXO* ended up being a "book of books," with eight separate, detailed sections, one for each major function inside a company. Each section was composed of several discrete short chapters outlining the key playbooks for each functional leadership role in the company. Because it covered CFOs, CMOs, CPOs, etc.--we landed on "Startup CXO" as the name. As a field guide, *Startup CXO* was massive—over 600 pages and 132 chapters and while we think the content is relevant to the entire leadership team, we recognize that a more focused book on each function is also something people need. The result is the book you have here, *Startup CRO: A Field Guide to Scaling up Your Company's Sales Function*, which is written for the current or aspiring Chief Revenue Officer who wants to know how to scale their function, wants to know what "great" looks like, and wants to work effectively with other members of the organization. As an added benefit, this book is shorter, easier to carry, and cheaper.

While the content in this book is largely the same as *Startup CXO*, we updated it and added several chapters on "How to Hire a CRO," and "How I Work With the Leadership Team." We also moved the chapters on Fractional work from *Startup CXO* to this book so that all of the relevant CRO information is in one book.

One major change we should note is a reflection of society: when we wrote *Startup CXO*, the pandemic was just underway and neither us nor anyone else could have predicted the impact globally, much less the drastic impact on startups and entrepreneurship. The impact of the pandemic on the world of work, in how business is conducted is well-known, from the great resignation to the permanence of remote work and hybrid models, but in the world of entrepreneurship the impact is less well-known. For example, in 2020 we wrote that "America's 'startup revolution' continues to gather steam" and noted that there are "increasing numbers of venture capital investors, seed funds, and accelerators supporting increasing numbers of entrepreneurial ventures." Today the world has changed, and while startup activity is still quite high, we are seeing more down-rounds, re-pricings, and recaps as venture capitalists are de-risking their investments. We're seeing expanding deal timelines and a focus on governance and accountability. Founders are likely to be operating under a microscope with less leeway, and with more scrutiny on management accountability and structures ensuring performance-based compensation. What that means for today's founders is that they need to develop a great organization right out of the gate, and that's where *Startup CRO* will come in handy.

While there are a number of books in the marketplace about CEOs and leadership, and some about individual functional disciplines (lots of books on the topic of Sales, the topic of Product Development, and the like), there are very few books that are practical how-to guides for any individual function, and that is where this series of "mini books" can help guide startup and scaleup teams. Each book in this series will serve as a how-to guide for a given executive, and taken together, the series will be a good how-to guide for startup executive teams in general. The five books are:

Finance and Administration
People and Human Resources
Marketing
Sales
Product and Engineering

We are starting with these "big five," but we may come back later and add to the series with Customer Success, Privacy, Business Development, and Operations, the other sections of *Startup CXO*.

This book carries my name as its principal author, and although I'm writing parts of it and editing it, I'm not THE author, I'm AN author. Anita Absey has been CRO at Return Path and Bolster and she is the principal author and the person who has the experience, credibility, and expertise to share something of value with others in the Sales organization. This material was also read and edited by additional CROs we know.

One caveat. Although this book is being written by Anita and me, it is not meant to be the Return Path story. We each have 20–30 years of experience working at multiple companies of different sizes and at different stages and in different sectors on which we are drawing. It's also not the story of Bolster, the new company that a number of us started during the pandemic in 2020. The book is based on our experience mostly in U.S.-based tech or tech-enabled services businesses, and more from the perspective of B2B than B2C, though inclusive of both. A few notes on language. We realize that not every leadership role in a startup is actually a "C"-level role. Sometimes the most senior person running a functional department is an SVP, a VP, a "head of," or even a Director or Manager. But Startup Functional Leader is a lousy title for a book. Regardless of title, we wrote with the most senior person responsible for the Sales organization in mind. Another point on terminology is that we use the words startup and scaleup in the book without precise revenue-based or employee-count-based definitions, but you should assume that startups are smaller companies, whereas scaleups are ones that have already reached some meaningful level of critical mass. We also use terms like "executive team," "leadership team," "C-suite," and "executive committee" interchangeably to refer to a company's senior-most group of leaders. Finally, we frequently refer to the concept of an "operating system." I talked about this at length in my earlier book, *Startup CEO*, but basically, it means––whether for a person, a team, or a company––the collection of meeting and communication routines and operating practices that form the cadence of a team's work.

Although the book is focused on the CRO role, there are insights for others in an organization. So, if you're a CEO, you could gain some additional insight into why something is not working in your sales organization––and understand how and what to change to create success in your sales team. I also have a "CEO-to-CEO Advice" section where I share my thoughts on what "great" looks like for the CRO, signs that your CRO isn't scaling, and how I engage with the CRO. I believe (and hope!) that CEOs, Board members, and investors can quickly get an overview and understanding of the CRO function by reading the "CEO-to-CEO Advice" chapter.

If you are a CRO or aspiring to become one, I hope this book speaks to you and inspires you in some way––that it's a playbook for something meaningful to you. If you're a CEO, maybe it will help you figure out who to hire or how to more effectively manage your CRO by telling you what "great" looks like for a CRO. If you're already a CRO in a startup, maybe it will help you focus on some aspect of your role you hadn't thought about yet. If you're an aspiring leader, maybe it will give you some insight into the kinds of steps you need to take in order to grow your career. Whichever persona you are, on behalf of me and Anita, we hope you gain some insight, and we thank you for reading *Startup CRO: A Field Guide to Scaling up Your Company's Sales Function.*

I. WELCOME TO THE EXECUTIVE TEAM

Matt Blumberg

Bolster Network

1

The Nature of a CXO's Role

I was struck by something as I read over the nearly complete manuscript of *Startup CXO* for the first time: each CXO believes that their part of the business is the most important part. And they make a compelling set of arguments:

Shawn: If you don't have a good product, you don't have a business.

Anita: If you don't have revenues, you don't have a business.

Ken: If you don't develop the ecosystem, you don't have a business.

Nick: If you don't generate market opportunities, you don't have a business.

George: If you don't create exceptional customer experiences, you don't have a business.

Cathy: If you don't recruit, train, and develop the right people, you don't have a business.

Jack: If you don't have the cash, you don't have a business.

Dennis: If you don't bake privacy in at the beginning, you don't have a business.

We had a debate years ago at a Return Path Board meeting as to whether we were a sales-driven business or a product-driven business—and more important, whether we should be one or the other.

Two of our Board members, both of whom I respect tremendously, were anchoring the different points of view, Scott Petry, on the product side, talking about how successful Apple was at getting customers to camp out overnight to be the first ones to buy the newest iThing; and Greg Sands, on the sales side, talking about how successful Oracle was at getting product into the hands of customers. I took a devil's advocate point of view in the conversation, true to our operating philosophy at Return Path, which was that HR/People was the most important function because we were a people-driven business.

So, who is right? Are the best companies sales-driven, product-driven, people-driven, or something else? Which of the CXO's functions is the most important? My answer is—they all are important, just in different ways, at different times, and in different combinations. While it's the CEO's job to balance the functions out—to figure out which lever to pull at which time, it's the CXO's job to be at the ready when their lever is pulled. And that gets to the important question of what the nature of a CXO role is, and why those roles can be tricky. CXOs have three principal jobs that they must keep in balance at all times, although there is a clear priority in my mind of the three jobs.

CXOs are first and foremost members of the company's Executive Team. They must, must, must put that team, understanding of the different functions, and the relationships on it at the top of their agenda. They shouldn't show up on the team only advocating for their own team. CEOs must insist on that behavior and mentality. Without it, a company simply can't function sustainably. This concept is one that we have always called the First Team concept, and it's articulated very eloquently by Patrick Lencioni in a number of his books, particularly in *The Five Dysfunctions of a Team* and *The Advantage*. As members of the Executive Team, all CXOs are accountable to each other for the success of the business as a whole and must partner with each other to achieve that success.

CXOs are also the head of their respective functional departments. They must carry the flag of their team and wave it proudly throughout the organization, especially when working with their teams. They are the functional role model, the functional mentor, and the functional decision-maker for the people on their functional team. To be an effective leader, they must be The Quintessential X (sales professional, engineer, marketer, etc.).

Finally, CXOs are company leaders. They are role models for company values. They should always be on alert for things that are going well or going poorly around them. Things that need attention or recognition. Situations that need calming down. Guests who are sitting unattended in the office lobby. Delivery people who need a check signed and who need to be tipped. Putting the new bottle of water onto the water cooler. You get the idea. Company leaders have the actual and moral authority to step outside of their departments and handle things as they need to be handled, regardless of which employees are involved.

2

Scaling a CRO

Congratulations, you just got promoted from Director of Sales to CRO! You're now in charge of a whole functional department, you now report to the CEO, you're now on the Executive Committee. You have a whole bunch of direct reports that either represent the team you used to lead or yesterday were your peers and you have now reached the pinnacle of your career in the Sales organization. The only other ways to grow your career vertically are to lead your function at a larger and larger company, or to become a CEO. Wow!

That feeling of euphoria is wonderful. I remember having it when I worked at MovieFone and became the head of marketing and product management instead of just the "Internet guy." It definitely led to a nice celebratory night out in Manhattan with friends.

But then, the reality set in the next morning. Uh oh. I've never done this job before. Maybe I know how to do 25% of it. I'm only 26 years old. Is anyone going to respect me? I have so much to learn. Can I fake it? How on earth did I find myself here? This phenomenon is called the Imposter Syndrome, and it's totally normal. In fact, if you grow your career quickly, it would be weird not to have at least a touch of it.

The good news is, you're not the first person to be promoted to an executive role for the first time (and of course you're not the last, either). Every single executive, at any company, had their first executive role at some point. While there's some credence to the expression "fake it till you make it," there's a more methodical approach you can take to scaling yourself as a CRO—or if you're the CEO, to helping your new CRO scale. Think of the journey in three steps that can be taken in any order.

First, master the tactics. You need to understand all of the things that happen in your department. Some you will know well because they're the ones you've done over time. Some you won't know at all. Make sure you do a complete inventory of the functional competencies for your role and all the roles reporting to you. Depending on how organized your company is with job descriptions and what's often known as a RACI (responsible-accountable-consulted-informed) analysis, this may be as easy as pulling something off the shelf and having a series of meetings with the people on your team to walk you through what they do. If your company isn't that organized, you may want to take the opportunity to proactively build that kind of functional competency/RACI list for everything in your team. That is no small exercise, but it's one that will pay back massive dividends. As Anita has often reminded me, "What gets measured gets managed." I'd add to that: if you don't know something even exists, you can't begin to measure it, let alone manage it!

Second, form your strategic approach. Every single function in a company has tactical and transactional elements to it—and every single function can be ONLY tactical if you let it. That's the lowest common denominator. HR can be about benefits and payroll. Sales can be about pipeline management and closing deals. Marketing can be about blog posts and SEO. A transactional focus is especially true of corporate functions like HR and Finance, but it's true of all functions. But just as every function has its tactical elements that must be attended to, every function CAN be strategic. As you settle into your new role, and as you grow into the role of senior executive and learn the First Team lesson of putting the needs of the business before the needs of your department, you will be able to start thinking more holistically about the business and how your department fits into it, so when your CEO pulls the lever that indicates they need your team to step up and lead, to be strategic on some topic, you are ready. What does it mean to be strategic vs. tactical? It's the difference between eating what's on your plate and planning out next week's menu. What are the ways in which the Sales organization can produce competitive differentiation for the business? What are the frameworks that will guide your decision-making about resource allocation or prioritization? How can you best support the other departments in the company? Those are the kinds of things you need to master in step 2. As my colleague Dave Wilby once said about one of the teams he was managing, "We have to figure out how to be the nose, not the tail."

Finally, look around the corner to see what's next for you and for your team. Senior executives constantly need to be toggling between different execution and planning horizons. You need to make your goals this quarter, and to make them, you have to hit daily or weekly activity metrics and milestones. But what about next quarter? Or next year? Or what happens if your company doubles in size in the next six months and is set to double again? Start by revisiting that functional competency/RACI list from step 1 and stress-test every element of it. Ask yourself, What must be true of this line item when the company is twice its current size? While you have to develop and scale as a leader—with all that goes into that in terms of soft skills—the only way to scale yourself as a CRO is to understand what great looks like for your role at the next stage of the company's life, and make sure you don't get there after your company needs you to.

All three of these steps—mastering the tactics of your department, forming your strategic approach, and understanding what's next—are things you may be able to do on your own to a point. That said, they will all go more quickly and with a higher probability of success if you engage your CEO, your Head of HR, members of your Board, or outside mentors or coaches to assist you on your journey.

II. CHIEF REVENUE OFFICER

Anita Absey and Matt Blumberg

Bolster Network

3

Chief Revenue Officer

Revenue to a company is fuel to a vehicle; it's air to an organism. It's the lifeblood of any successful company. Can you get by without revenue? For a while, but sooner or later you have to figure out how to generate revenue and, more importantly, figure out why you can't. The time to do all this figuring is in the very early stages of your startup, like week 1.

You should immediately dismiss the notion that "if you build it, people will love it and buy it." It's difficult to dismiss that kind of thinking because a lot of founding teams have spent months, years, and even decades developing a product; they have put all their savings into the startup; they have tapped their friends, relatives, and possibly angel and venture capital investors. I appreciate that effort and risk, but falling in love with your technology, product, or service doesn't matter. What matters is whether or not you have something people want to buy.

Loving Your Technology...And Losing The Sale

A while ago I went to buy a car and I found one that I absolutely loved. I loved the feel of it, I loved driving it, I loved the whole experience of it. When I got back to the dealership, the salesperson

> opened the hood and started talking to me about the horsepower, the torque, and other performance features. He lost me, and he lost the sale. Why? He didn't understand what I valued about the car and his focus on the car (the product) and its features were important to him but not to me. **Anita Absey**

As a startup, you need to understand how potential customers value your product. Does it save them time? Is it a better solution to something they need? Is it more cost-effective? The way to go about this is to get out in the world and talk to customers. In the very early stages you'll most likely explore and validate your product with the CEO and Head of Product. But to scale, you'll need to develop processes, systems, and hire and develop a team. In this book I share ways for you to build a great Sales Organization.

4

In the Beginning

From Prospect to Customer

There's a framework that Matt borrowed from one of our original investors at Return Path, Greg Sands. Greg always talked about the evolution of an enterprise selling process as going from "selling on white-board" (a largely custom and conceptual sale) to "selling with PowerPoint" (a sale that requires creativity and tailored pitches) to "selling with PDF" (a standard sale that can be taught quickly to an inexperienced sales rep and used with a high degree of predictability to all customers). Part of what that means is that, as a startup, your goal is not to deliver a polished, final PDF to customers, something that is buttoned down and refined, but to start with a mindset of discovery. As the Chief Revenue Officer, along with your CEO and maybe Head of Product, you should go to a prospect's office and literally use a whiteboard, drawing things out, drawing charts and frameworks and circles and arrows and exclamation points, while you try to understand your potential customer's problem and then go back to the office and work on building the solution they need. You're creating this with the client because you don't have a deck yet, much less a PDF. You've got your initial product, but you're still very much in discovering and positioning mode. You are an evangelist. You don't know what resonates in your prospect's mind. It can be very interactive and engaging with you selling on a whiteboard and using that very intimate moment to try to develop the right story for your product.

Then, as you evolve and grow, chances are you are going to have a sales deck and a pitch because you won't be discovering what the customer needs, but you'll have very refined (and tested) ideas about their needs, maybe even customer segments. But a caution here is that what could and often does happen is that your deck, your pitch, gets modified along the way—for every single pitch. So, if you have four salespeople, each of them has a different version on their laptop, and there's probably no central organizing body yet that has thought about what the tone and tenor of the brand should be. This stage is called "Selling with PowerPoint" because good, clever, senior, business development-oriented salespeople are most successful by creating custom pitches for each client based on their learned history of what has and has not worked in other places. You're lucky if sales reps share their knowledge and slides across the group. You are still miles away from being a sales machine.

What you want to strive for is a level of sophistication and market understanding that enables you to get to a PDF presentation. A PDF is something that's complete, that can't be modified or altered, and it ensures that everyone's speaking the same language. At this point you have the kind of consistency and message and positioning that enable you to be repeatable and scalable. Obviously selling by whiteboard—and even PowerPoint—is sufficient to a point in time but if you're thinking about unleashing your product on a massive scale, then you have to get to the point where you have a very smooth presentation and message that you know resonates with the audience.

Once you have the consistent, polished PDF, you might think that all you have to do as your company scales is to use that and tweak it a bit here or there for particular customers. That could work, but sometimes the best way to sell is not to use materials. Sometimes, if salespeople rely on that magic piece of collateral or the better deck, they actually miss the point: you want your salespeople to connect with the customer, to discover with the customer, and you want them to understand the customer's problems. A great salesperson needs to constantly hone their questioning and discovery skills and that's what you ought to look for when hiring and building your sales team.

A great salesperson also needs to be able to ask questions that allows them to understand when a "no" is really a "no." There's a common belief among salespeople that "a quick 'no' can often be better than a long 'yes'." Although there are a lot of people who do believe that, I reject that thinking. A quick "no" is an easy way out for a salesperson, especially if they're dealing with a qualified prospect. But I would say that you should only accept "no" if you feel as though you've gotten an honest response to important discovery questions, after you've had a chance to paint a picture of what success looks like.

A salesperson needs to be able to discern whether a response by a potential customer is a brush-off—or is it legitimate? Or are they getting a response like "we don't have time," or "we don't have the budget," or "we don't have the need"? Getting to an honest, legitimate "no" quickly is better than a long protracted "no," but it's more nuanced than what most people think and it requires probing and thoughtful questions from the salesperson. It also depends on the product or solution sales cycle but, as long as you're in control of the process and you can accurately forecast your pipeline, then a long "no" is fine. A warning here, though: if your sales cycle turns out to be 18 months, then even if you have 25 "yes's," you better find a way to get companies where you have higher appeal because you'll starve waiting for those to come in.

You might be thinking that you can get your sales team from white-board to PDF quickly, that it's a matter of understanding the process and then executing it. But the reality is that there is no quick way to get from whiteboard to PDF and it's not a linear process. You can't put into your business plan that you'll spend the first six months selling with whiteboard, the next six months selling with PowerPoint, and the next six months selling with PDF. It's much more nuanced, there's a lot of trial and error, a lot of experimentation, and a lot of thinking and rethinking based on customer ideas and feedback. At Return Path, for example, it probably took us somewhere between five to ten years before we got from whiteboard to PDF and it was only after refining our approach and materials that we were able to build a sales machine.

5

Hiring the Right People

In the beginning, as you're discovering more about your product and solution, you'll go on calls with the CEO and others at your company and eventually, you'll do that yourself. Once you validate your model, you might think that you're ready to hire, but a good practice is to set a reasonable stretch goal in the beginning, like 25 customers using the product within three months, or even ten customers. You are the first salesperson, of course, and you won't be able to hire additional people until you really understand your products and customers. So, while you might believe that you can hire a salesperson quickly, it's better to err on caution and make sure you're very clear on your product, solution, competitive alternatives, pricing, and customer benefits before hiring your first salesperson.

Once you hit that target, you'll be ready to hire salespeople to help you, but who do you hire, and how do you figure out if they will be good at sales, especially if you're in a new market? You might think that hiring someone fresh out of college is the way to go, that a young person will grow with the business. Certainly, there are a lot of talented people with college degrees from first-rate universities, and while we appreciate what it takes to get into a highly competitive university, the intelligence and work ethic required. But for a startup, it's more important to find people who understand the nuance of selling, who can listen, who can understand other people, and who can tell a story, a narrative. The best salespeople often are the people who have faced and overcome adversity or failure—maybe financially, maybe in their relationships, maybe in a previous job—because those people will have higher empathy for others, and that's what you need to be successful in Sales.

In terms of hiring salespeople, it's difficult to create an interview process that hits on all the important points, but there are a few points that are critical to get a handle on early when you interview candidates. Obviously, you should certainly be interested in a person's expertise and experience. Beyond that, you would want to know whether or not you successfully made quota, carried a bag, and in what verticals you've been successful. You'd want to hear about your success stories but also want to know what you've learned from failure. You don't want to just focus on the art of selling, but you also want to know if someone is focused on the math of selling because you need both—you need the empathy and listening skills, and you need to be process-oriented and deliberate and organized in your approach to building a pipeline and moving things through the pipeline and forecasting.

It's not easy to ask questions that will direct you to those answers. But it's easy to have a conversation about things like, What is most important to you? What do you think is the most important part of the sales process? How do you manage yourself so that you can manage the process? What kinds of questions do you ask customers or prospects about business as part of a discovery?

These are very simple broad questions that if someone is really trying to be successful or has been successful in sales, they'll be able to answer, effortlessly. We can say that with confidence because we've seen it when it works. And we can know in five minutes if it doesn't work.

You might be tempted to create a fake sales situation for a candidate, thinking that you'll get a better sense of their ability than by asking them a series of questions. It's very difficult to create a realistic sales situation since there's so much nuance and listening involved. It's artificial. But we have done that and can recommend two approaches that go beyond interviewing. One way to approach it is to test whether the sales candidate has done enough work researching your organization to be able to craft some potential discovery questions. So, one way to stress test a candidate is by asking them to imagine that you are a potential customer of Return Path (or whatever company you are hiring for). How would they begin the conversation with you? In doing this, you can learn if they have the right discovery questions. Have they done their homework?

Another way to vet candidates beyond interviewing is to say to the person, "I have someone equally as qualified as you for this role. Please tell me why I should select you." And that very often flusters people but if you can't sell yourself with confidence, then you're probably not going to be able to sell a solution.

One final thing on hiring. It's important to have people from different functions in the company interview the salesperson because a salesperson needs to work well with others—the product team, the marketing team, the technology team, the finance team. You can be sure that if a salesperson is going to be demanding of these groups, which inevitably they are, then there absolutely has to be a natural sense that this person is a collaborator and not a demander and that they will bring ideas back into the organization. So, getting perspectives from different departments is critical. It could be a big mistake to hire someone who ticks all the sales boxes but is not well received by others in the company.

Hire With Head Or Heart?

In hiring salespeople, sometimes you go with your heart, not your head. Of course, you consider someone's experience and expertise and prior success—but it may be their passion, their heart, and their genuine enthusiasm that will triumph, even if they may not have the polish or demeanor you hope for. One of the best hires I ever made was very successful by sheer force of will, good humor, creativity, and persistence ... despite being a bit rough around the edges. He looked more like a disheveled radical than a business person, but he was one of the best salespersons I ever hired.

Sometimes, despite all of your assessments, interviews, and reference checks, you make a big mistake, and that is time-consuming and costly. My worst experience was hiring someone who ticked all the right boxes, and in hindsight, maybe too well, and too smoothly. We found out within a few months of hiring them that they actually had taken another job at another company at the same time and were attempting to work for both while "calling in sick" or "working remotely" half of the time. We immediately terminated them but lost time spent in onboarding, training, and quota attainment. My only counsel here is when you make a mistake, correct it as soon as possible, whether it is in an unusual situation like this, or whether someone is clearly not succeeding in the early days. **Anita Absey**

Profile of Successful Salespeople

There are a lot of misperceptions about salespeople—and no wonder, there are so many types of sales approaches, and we've all experienced being "sold" that it's easy to think of sales as "convincing people to buy something they really don't want." Nothing could be further from the truth. A great salesperson has to lead with empathy and have a real interest in helping others solve their problems. This is difficult for some people to understand, especially people with a product that solves problems, but even though a successful salesperson is a solutions seller, they're not doing that from their point of view, but from the customer's point of view. A great salesperson can paint a picture of a future state and bring the prospect along on the journey by asking questions and helping them to understand impact, value, and outcomes.

Most importantly, a great salesperson is not a talker, but a listener, and they listen for understanding and comprehension. Yes, a great salesperson deeply understands the product, but they're not focused on features and functions, like the car salesperson referenced earlier. Instead, they're focused on the benefit and advantages to the prospect. But first and foremost, they have excellent listening skills and even more broadly, the ability to understand visual cues from customer interactions. Does the salesperson notice that the potential customer is getting bored, is not paying attention, or is anxious? Those are cues that a good salesperson will recognize and rather than keep talking, maybe wrap up a conversation.

Sales is a process and discipline, as well as an art. A good salesperson will understand and use the "sales math" that gets you from first call to cash. That means they'll know how many phone calls they'll have to make each day to get a customer to respond; how many responses they'll need to get a customer to agree to a meeting; how many meetings they'll need to get a customer to say "yes." A great salesperson will always have this calculation in mind, they'll know where they are in the process, and they'll be able to lean in, give more effort to the right areas, so that they can hit their weekly, monthly, or quarterly targets.

A Good Hiring Model

There was a good hiring model we adopted at Return Path at the suggestion of a private equity investor. We looked for sales candidates early in their career, who were successful at selling commodity products, and who were likely not from top tier universities. The thought was that if they could sell a commodity, they would be able to connect with prospects, and could be taught how to sell a more complex solution. We also believed that they would fight harder to win, as they may not have had the educational pedigree that made it easy for them to land a plum role. There was an assessment that we did as part of the interview process, and if the candidate passed that (a must), and did well in the interview process, then they were likely a good hire. This does presume though, that you have a sales trainer and training program to help them develop solution-selling skills. This proved to be a good way to "grow our own" team, and took some of the risk out of the onboarding process and improved the time-to-value period. **Anita Absey**

If you can create a model of the qualities needed to be a successful salesperson in your organization, that is the surest way to hire the right people. If you can't (yet) create that model, then search for people who have high integrity, a zest for success personally and professionally, perseverance, and persistence. These are critical traits that I look for in potential candidates and salespeople with these traits can be successful in most situations.

One word of caution: the characteristics that define a successful salesperson can be very different than what is needed in a Sales Manager or leader. A successful salesperson has to be an excellent communicator and listener, self-motivated (and self-interested to some extent), and inspired by the chase and the win. The sales manager should have those skills but also the ability to coach and mentor, to manage performance, and provide strategic guidance. Those additional qualities are critical in the successful sales manager. A leader will set the tone and tenor for the organization, embodying the vision and mission for the team, and inspiring high standards of performance and accountability.

Some Myth Busting

Here are some common misperceptions about salespeople:

- They are only motivated by money.

- They sell primarily based on relationships, dinners, drinks, and false promises. (I say never let the relationship get in the way of revenue.)

- A successful salesperson is the lone wolf.

- Successful salespeople are extroverts who have to be in control of the conversation.

- The successful salesperson talks endlessly about product features and functions.

- The successful salesperson has a deep, extensive, rolodex of contacts and customers.

All of these ideas listed above are not true of great sales organizations—although they are true of some people, some cultures, and some organizations. But for great sales organizations, they're misperceptions, they're ideas that people have about salespeople. As a CRO, if you believe these ideas, then you'll recruit based on them, and that's what you'll populate your Sales team with. And then you'll naturally talk about salespeople as extroverts motivated by money and needing to control the conversation. That's not a recipe for success, that's not conducive to a successful sales culture. A successful sales culture is one of sharing ideas with others on the team, mentoring others to build a stronger team, listening to the customer rather than telling them about products and features, and building a relationship of trust with the customer through empathy.

It's likely within a startup that other members of the executive team will have these same misperceptions of salespeople and one of the first things you can do is to educate them on what a successful sales team is. If someone on your executive teams says something like "Well, salespeople are only motivated by money," you'll have to be direct: "No, that's a misperception and I'm building a sales team culture that will out-perform any team focused only on financial motivations." The time to set the stage for the culture you want to build is Day 1, not 18 months into your startup, and in doing that, you'll set your company up for growth.

Compensating Sales Team Members

Of all the myths surrounding salespeople, the one that is most widely accepted is that salespeople are wholly driven by money, which is not necessarily true. But compensation is a big part of building a sales team and it's one of the areas you'll have to think about early in your startup and revisit over time as you scale. Often, two things occur in startups that you have to watch out for. One is that you hire someone who's willing, and enjoys the chase. You know they're motivated and they'll be aggressive but there's so much uncertainty that it doesn't make sense to have commissions. So, you pay that person an inflated salary, noting for them that part of their salary will eventually be turned into an incentive compensation. The challenge there is that it's very hard to dial back money once you put it out there. And even if you're explicit about it, even if you have it written down, the salesperson is likely to view any reduction in salary as a negative. So that is not a preferred form.

The preferred form of incentive in a startup is to give someone an aggressive salary, something that is at or above market. You want (and need) to get the best salespeople in your company, so pay for it. Don't try to go in on the cheap. That never works. Pay for the talent you think is going to help you be successful, based on market rates, and then pay a high flat commission rate on every single dollar that comes in the door. Our advice is always the same for a pure startup: when you're just getting out there, $0-10 million in revenues, pay everyone a commission on every single dollar.

$10 million might be too high for many companies, but pick your number so that it's appropriate for your finances, cash position, speed of the sales cycle, or other factors unique to you. But sales incentive compensation is critically important. It's one way to absolutely influence the behavior of someone on your team. As you get a little more mature, a leveraged plan where you pay a high variable rate and a lower base salary works well. A good approach is to base compensation on a quarterly target because it's easier for people to have something in their line of vision. And as the CRO, it allows you to adjust for seasonality as appropriate. So, if my quota is a million dollars a year, I'm overwhelmed, but if I have to hit $250k this quarter, I know exactly (if I know my sales math) how many calls I have to make and how many meetings I have to set up to get to close, based on the conversion rate. That's an easier number to think about!

With a quarterly plan you'd want to pay people increasing amounts based on them getting closer to their target. Maybe you'd have tiers or bands of $0–25,000, $25,000–50,000 or whatever is appropriate, but you'd pay them a higher commission rate as they go through those tiers. So, they're really rewarded for getting that business and for pulling things into the current quarter. Once your salespeople meet 100% of their target, it's appropriate to offer additional incentives based on the incremental dollars that come in, above goal.

It's important to have incentive plans with no caps, so that you do not diminish the earning potential of anyone on the team. This rewards attainment, and emphasizes the fact that the company is willing to pay for high performance, regardless of how high the commission payout may be (See also Chapter 18).

One caution: Avoid applying incentives that encourage reps to pull deals into a quarter at a discount. This diminishes your value proposition, and sets the expectation in the market that you will play on price to close business.

There are obviously a lot of ways to compensate and motivate salespeople, but having a clear plan early in a startup and recognizing the potential for growth will lead to better results and also reduce turnover, which can be a huge problem in a sales organization.

Incentive Compensation Revisited

Evolving Your Compensation Plans

When you're expanding, you're beyond the startup phase and you'll probably need to revisit your incentive compensation plans. Like other elements of the sales organization, you'll outgrow what worked in the early days and it's far better to be proactive rather than reactive. This is especially true for incentive compensation since it's a key motivational driver within the sales organization.

As a startup and as you're scaling, I believe that a flat percentage for every dollar of bookings is what works best. As you expand, you'll want to leverage the incentive plan with escalating percentages as a salesperson gets closer to their annual number. I suggest quarterly targets because it's easier for a salesperson to determine the number of calls, the number of meetings, etc. that they have to do to hit a quarterly target. And, yes, the clock goes back to zero after each quarter so that also motivates the salesperson to be sure that they're constantly building their pipeline. You want them not only to be working in the current quarter, but also to be thinking about how to keep building the pipeline as they're closing deals. That takes a lot of discipline and a lot of coaching from you, the CRO. A good compensation plan will help people figure out how to do that, how to pull things in from the quarter ahead so they can get the higher percentage. They'll want to make sure their pipeline is always robust.

Once you're beyond startup, the processes around onboarding become much more important. You'll have a differentiated market, buyer segments, personas, and verticals, so your sales team members will vary based on experience and sophistication. You'll need to hire more team members and as you do that, since your company and markets are more complex, you'll have to onboard new people. The length of your onboarding depends on how quickly a person can become fluent in asking the questions, following the sales methodology, and assimilating your sales philosophy. Obviously, you want that time to be as compressed as possible so their time to value is 60 days rather than 120 days.

For that first quarter, rather than have a salesperson starve, you might consider paying them on achieving other goals, like completing any number of trainings, going on X sales calls, and beginning to develop some pipeline. Your onboarding should have as its goal a series of buildable skills so that new hires don't lose their zeal to be successful in subsequent quarters. A non-recoverable draw for the first 90 days is possible too, especially if you have a complex business. The risk is that you lose that money, but if a person doesn't hit these early goals, you're probably better off letting them go after 90 days. Hopefully you made a better hiring decision so that doesn't occur. If it does happen, you may want to revisit your hiring practices.

Incentive compensation plans, like all of the elements in the sales organization, have to evolve as you scale and expand. If you don't constantly upgrade them, you'll find yourself flatfooted in the market and scrambling to catch up.

9

Pipeline

Two of the biggest sales challenges in a startup involve pipeline and forecasting because there are so many unknowns. Pipeline and forecasting are different processes and require different skills and you should develop models and ideas about them separately. There are a lot of companies that make both pipeline and forecasting so complex with lots of details, metrics, and analytics, but they still can't get a strong pipeline, nor can they develop accurate forecasts. Creating a pipeline is not something to be done within the silo of Sales, it takes collaboration with Marketing, with Business Development if you have that function, with Product, and with Finance. With so many people involved, it's important to have a system of record, be it Salesforce.com or HubSpot or something else, but you absolutely need to have a place that's a central repository of information.

In the beginning you need to begin collecting data to understand exactly what the dynamics of your pipeline are. Even if that information is incorrect to start, trying to map out a pipeline framework to your buyer's journey is critical. What data is important? Information from your buyers about their decision-making processes, about timing, about how they evaluate products is a good place to start. You need to think about your activity but also how that activity influences the buyer, what it is that's affecting their journey. Of course, you can assign probabilities to each of those stages and you'll begin to develop some well-worn pipeline management paths. But in the early days it's important to at least start with a framework, because if you don't know where you're going, everything you do will be inefficient and ineffective.

The other questions to ask prospects in addition to decisions, timing, and evaluation, are almost mentor-like questions and if you've developed a relationship with the customer, they will help you by answering them. You should ask questions like, "What will help us get to the next step? What things should I be considering?" It takes a lot of boldness and courage to ask those questions and the buyer might not even know the answers, but you form that together.

As an early stage startup, you're working with so little, but it doesn't take very long to develop a philosophy, a theory, about what's the right entry and exit criteria, to develop several paths that, with your probabilities, tell you something important about how well you'll close deals. And if you use data historically as you go forward, you'll be able to see how a deal closed, how many days were in each stage. So, when something comes up, like this deal was lost in the fourth stage, you'll be able to figure out if you should have spent more time in the early discovery stages.

As a startup, you may have only one customer type but as you grow, you'll find that you have segments, you have different buyer journeys, and maybe different experiences with your product based on region, vertical, or some other factors. But you absolutely have to start understanding your pipeline, you have to understand things like days and stage and time to close so you can improve your pipeline management and, ultimately, your forecasting. Probably the most potent combination of art and science that exists in the whole revenue process is understanding how to manage your pipeline and how you can tie that to accurate forecasting.

The major differentiator between the startup that is struggling and the startup that is poised to scale is pipeline management and forecasting.

10

Scaling the Sales Organization

We would not suggest scaling (from a revenue perspective) until you have a consistent viewpoint of the buyers of your product or service. If you're still at the whiteboard stage, no matter how passionate and optimistic you are about the future, it will be difficult to scale. You'll need to be at the PowerPoint stage if you want to scale. You should have answers to questions on the buyer's problems, you should have a good understanding of the competitive landscape and where you fit, you should have a philosophy on your value, and you should have a methodology that allows you to know where you're at in the pipeline and what's forecast in the future. Without a solid understanding of these basic elements, scaling is just a pipe dream.

In the very, very early stages of a company, when you haven't stratified to the point where you have enterprise sales or small and medium-sized business (SMB) sales, you'll have all those sales in one person or possibly in one "type" of sales rep—people who are jacks of all trades. If you have a person who is a go-getter and they can tell the story as an entrepreneur, they will likely have the ability to close large enterprise deals and to speak to mid-market. As the CRO, you should make sure that they can close business in all those segments to feed your enterprise. You'll probably find that smaller sales happen quicker than enterprise sales, but you should validate that with your business. The worst thing, the last thing you want, is an enterprise-level effort for a transactional sale. So, you have to be sure to balance all of that but also carefully map retention rates by segment.

As you start to scale, you'll have a lot of things in place that you worked on as a startup, for example, you ought to have a pretty good idea about the type of person that's best suited to be in your organization. You should have your hiring profile done so that you can just turn on that machine and always be hiring. You never want to fall behind in sales power because if someone walks out the door, even though you have a pipeline, you don't want to be surprised with a departure and then have to say, "We just lost that quota." You want to be sure you have a deep enough bench to allow for any kind of voluntary or involuntary exits from the organization and you can accomplish this in two ways. You can either have more junior people who can be promoted to carry more quota, or you can have more quota in your existing pipeline. Either way, you don't want a sudden departure to shove the sales organization off the rails. You'll also have to be thoughtful about career-pathing as you scale.

Ideas on Career Paths

I currently work with ethics compliance software and we've found different tiers of the market, different appeal of the product to small and medium-sized business, and different appeal than what we see at the enterprise level. If you can match the market segment by the type of salesperson, you can create career paths that provide growth opportunities for them and reduce turnover for you. So, you might have someone early in their career focus on the SMB mid-market because they may not have developed the sophistication and expertise to appropriately handle a larger enterprise sale that may go across many divisions and even into the C-level. And an entry-level salesperson with no prior experience I'd start out as a sales development rep (SDR) doing inside sales. Sometimes an SDR is housed within Marketing and sometimes Sales, but that's a good place for inexperienced people to start to learn the sales methodology, process, math, and approach. **Anita Absey**

To really be able to scale, you'll need to have a profile of the people you want to hire, and a career path for them to follow. Without those, you're likely to spend a lot of time looking for people, in part because you don't know what you're looking for and in part because you'll have a lot of turnover in the sales organization.

Don't Blindly Promote Your Best Salesperson

There is often a classic mistake made by sales leaders (and this happened to me), where you promote your best salesperson into a sales management role, and it turns into an epic fail. In my case, the salesperson insisted that management was the next best, and only desired, step in their career. At the risk of having them leave the organization, I put them in a sales management role, despite my misgivings.

Within months, we lost some quality members from their team—they were just not a good manager, coach, or mentor. Eventually, (finally) we made the decision to let them go as well, so the outcome was bad for them, for team morale, and for the company.

My guidance here would be to craft an interesting career path for people who stay in an independent contributor role. This could mean having them take on more strategic enterprise accounts as their career progresses, or creating a Global Account Management role that spans geographies, and provides an opportunity to lead and collaborate with teams internally to successfully penetrate and manage global accounts with multiple subsidiaries. The important point is to match impact with expertise, and to reward and recognize those who choose sales, and not management, as a career path.

At the end of the day, have the corporate courage to "just say no," when someone is not a good fit for a role, and move on. The long-term benefits will far outweigh any short-term pain. **Anita Absey**

11

Scaling Your Team Through Culture

Your team will scale naturally as you grow and by that I mean, you'll hire people based on what works for your company, and based on the growth rate of the company. When you think of scaling your team, think of creating the type of sales culture that will allow your team to scale—not so much just hiring more people, but hiring people who make a big impact in the company in the way that fits with your company values. If you build the right sales culture first, then you can spend your time proactively building the pipeline rather than reactively solving internal problems. You create this impactful sales organization through your management, your systems, and your culture. The sales culture is the essence of a good sales organization and that means having an organization where everyone is holding themselves and one another to really high standards of performance and accountability.

There are a lot of companies that subscribe to a productive competition mindset as a way to motivate salespeople, to focus them on getting their quota, making their numbers. That works to some extent, but it's more effective to reward performance through recognition. For example, it's possible to create standard awards for recognition and even crowdsourcing awards among the team so that you are recognizing performance, like biggest deal to close, breakthrough in a new industry, whatever it might be. This is different than making it competitive among the sales team members.

There are some sales organizations that create a President's Club, with trips to island paradise resorts for the winners, but that ends up fostering competition among the team, it's elitist and it doesn't play well to the company as a whole. If you have a President's Club for Sales, what about Engineering or HR? As leaders where the executive team is the first team, we don't like it. There are other organizations that pay spiffs, where a salesperson gets an additional amount of money if they facilitate a particular product. Yes, you can drive some top-line growth that way but you're not helping the sales team to focus on the buyer's problem, they're just getting some extra money for selling something the product team rolled out.

Avoid Special Treatment

> At Return Path, we created something called "Performance As-pire," which recognized (with relevant data) our highest performers from across all departments in the organization, and could include up to 100 people from around the globe. We held a single big event that included recognition, but also coaching, mentoring, and information-sharing opportunities. The feedback from across the organization was positive, and something that people "aspired" to attain as part of their time with Return Path (See also *Startup Chief People Officer* for a fuller discussion or rewards and recognition).
> **Anita Absey**

But, as CRO you may have situations where you recognize that you're having a down quarter or you feel as if people just need to feel some level of enthusiasm, need to be jazzed up for whatever reason. A way to motivate the sales team if there are across-the-board problems is to provide a public spiff and tie it to the pipeline. Give everyone some type of reward as you *approach* your goals—don't wait until you hit them. You could call it a sales contest, for example, who can close the most accounts? Who can make the most calls today, or have the most meetings, or create the most pipeline this week? Hopefully, the work that you're doing as part of your CRO day-to-day workload management would eliminate the need for that, but it can be helpful, especially when markets are impacting your entire organization.

So, there is a role for awards, for recognition, and for spiffs in a sales organization, but those tools are really managing by exception. Instead, if you want to build a great sales organization, focus on creating a culture of transparency, of sharing, and learning. The best salespeople can learn from one another rather than compete with one another. They can learn from their managers, customers, and prospects, and they can share that with their colleagues. To build a great sales organization, create an environment of ongoing learning and continuous process improvement, not a cut-throat environment, but one that's highly, highly accountable for performance, highly recognized and rewarded for performance, or one that also inspires a sense of common purpose and collaboration.

Help People Become Successful

As the CRO, creating this type of culture starts with you, starts with how you interact with others in your organization. I (Anita) learned an important lesson early on in my sales management career, from someone who had been a peer, and was now one of my direct reports. As I was consistently asking Ronda whether she had included certain information, or talking points for an important presentation, to Fidelity Investments, and making endless suggestions for change, she suggested that I trust her to do her job, and that she wanted this opportunity as much as I did.

I realized then that the most effective way to manage and develop people is to work through them to make them successful. It does not matter how much I know, or how well I can do something—it matters that I use that to help others become successful. Work through others to ensure their success, and my own. **Anita Absey**

In managing a sales organization you'll certainly look at the numbers, but it's not just about the numbers. You don't want a brilliant jerk in the organization, a star performer who treats other people without a level of respect. Similarly, someone who's really nice but is not a performer is not someone to continue with the organization either.

Lone Wolf or Team Player?

I noted earlier that there is a myth that the "Lone Wolf" is often the most successful salesperson. Actually, that may often be true in terms of putting numbers on the board, but is often not true when considering the rest of the organization. For example, here's a situation I had that's quite common for the CRO: I had an extremely capable performer who consistently met and exceeded quota expectations, but was roundly disliked by many of the people with whom they had to collaborate. They showed a lack of respect for other people's time and responsibilities, often ran over people to get their items to the top of an agenda (be it in Product or Marketing), and failed to acknowledge or show appreciation for the support they were getting from others that helped make them successful. They clearly were not a good culture fit, and that was corrosive. Despite multiple conversations about working well with others to get things done, we eventually had to exit them from the organization. For me, WHAT you do and HOW you do it are equally important. Just hitting your numbers is not enough if you go about it in a disruptive way.
Anita Absey

When a CRO has to provide feedback, a best practice is ensure that the feedback be directed toward helping a salesperson understand your philosophy because that's where the breakdown for most sales behaviors happen. For example, good feedback is typically around helping the salesperson to look "outside in" and not to fall into the trap of talking about our product. That stems from a philosophy that a good sales organization conducts sales with empathy and understanding of the buyer. It's a constant, as a CRO, to remind your sales team to be looking at our company through the customer's eyes. There are software tools that allow you to listen to a sales rep's call and help you analyze and understand how much talking the salesperson did versus the prospect. That provides analytic insight to the salesperson and to the manager and helps each strive for continuous improvement.

That type of feedback can really help a salesperson refine their communications and help them understand if they are asking questions and listening as opposed to just talking. As CRO, you want your salespeople talking about customer problems and how you solve them. You should want your sales team to get the buyer to the point where they're actually thinking that they're controlling the sale, even though the salesperson is controlling it through their questions positioned in the right way. That's the feedback we would provide, given our sales philosophy.

So, a powerful sales culture is one that has at its root an environment of constant coaching, mentoring, support, and encouragement with standards, not an environment of fear. A great sales organization will not be punitive but will have high standards and high emotional IQ as well. And if you can create a safe environment, where people can openly discuss, disagree, and share, then you'll have an environment where feedback is welcome, where feedback is recognized as a gift. When you get that, you can scale as quickly as the market will allow.

There are other sales cultures that are effective, however, and the choice is up to you. You can be successful, for example, by running a boiler room that churns and burns out people and customers. You'll have a lot of conflict and, most likely, low morale. It's not a fun way to spend the day for you or your sales organization, it's not sustainable, it doesn't really develop people, and it's not sophisticated. The approach we advocate, what we believe a great sales organization will embrace, is the opposite of that in all respects. We choose to invest in people, to encourage them, to create a space for sharing and learning. But, different industries have different characteristics, and ultimately the choice is yours.

12

Scaling Sales Process and Methodology

When you're scaling your sales organization, you should have a very good handle on your sales processes and methodology. It's wise to embrace some type of sales methodology, to have something that enables you to have a framework you work from. You should have a common language around the buyer's journey, and how that aligns with the stages in the pipeline. Otherwise, it's going to be very hard to develop a consistent point of view across the organization about what works and what doesn't work. The sales methodology will help guide the way you question and move the sale along, and the concept of the buyer's journey will enable you to understand how the buyer is looking at you and how that aligns with what must be true for you to come in and out of a pipeline stage.

In the very early stages, when you're selling on whiteboard and you're just trying to get business, developing a sales methodology will be difficult because there are too many unknowns. But as you close in on a few million dollars in sales, when you really need to think about scaling, that's when a methodology is important. You'll be able to ask questions like, why is something getting stuck in evaluation? Or worse, why is something stuck in negotiation when it has sped through the evaluation stage? Clearly you didn't do your homework early on, you didn't think about the methodology and asking the kinds of questions that would have helped you understand the problem, and be able to understand the gap between the problem and the solution you fill with your product or technology.

As you scale, your methodology will expand, it will evolve to include more scenarios that impact both the sales organization and the rest of the company. In the early stages, for example, you might sell to every customer that you can but when you're scaling, you will have figured out the effort and payoff of certain customers and you'll be able to resist selling to everybody and only sell to the most profitable customers. In the beginning you might have the philosophy that "the customer is always right." It's not true that the customer is always right and there are situations where a salesperson is dealing with a very, very demanding customer. In that instance, it's helpful to coach the salesperson to ask questions to discover those demands, to make sure that they're having a conversation with the customer and letting them know that we are here as a partner to provide a solution. Our approach is to do that in an environment of mutual respect and understanding.

In a really difficult situation, if a customer undermines our salesperson, or shows a lack of respect or takes advantage of someone in the company, then that's not a positive relationship and you should be willing to happily walk away from that if it's not tenable. People are eminently reasonable and if you try to understand where they're coming from, and what's motivating their demands, potentially you can find a solution. But not always.

At Return Path we did have one customer who was downright rude and threatening to one of our salespeople, and we fired the customer. I made a call to Matt, and he responded with "There's no place for this, our people aren't going to get treated like that. The negative to our culture isn't worth the positive of that one contract." So, your sales methodology is more than a selling process, it also informs what you don't want to do, what customers you don't want to have.

Your Methodology Determines Your Actions

You can also run into a situation, anytime in your growth, where your methodology compels you to do something you'd rather not do. Very early on at Return Path, we chased a high-profile, fast-growing phenomenon and we had a salesperson on it, but because it was an important multi-million dollar deal we also brought in Matt to help close it. At one point during negotiations they demanded (and we reluctantly agreed to give them) most favored nation pricing which is something I loathe because it's just a race to the bottom. We carved out a couple of exceptions that had been longstanding in the US and as we were negotiating the final deal, someone from the Finance team came to me and said, "Anita, I'm sorry. I made a mistake when I gave you the carve-outs for the agreement. I forgot to include company XYZ."

I said, "OK, that's fine. No problem. Thank you for owning up to the mistake." I went to Matt and told him we made a mistake and the result would be $250,000 to the good for the client (meaning $250,000 to the bad for us). I said to Matt, "I think that we should live by our values and we should do the right thing." He responded, "Absolutely. Of course." And with that I went to our customer and I said, "John, we made an error in your favor and I want you to know this will be the hallmark of how we work together. One of our credos is to do the right thing and when we found out about the $250,000 mistake, we felt we had to honor our agreement." He literally signed the agreement that day and instantly became a huge advocate for us and a reference customer based on how we handled the situation.

Anita Absey

Your methodology is at first about customer discovery, understanding their journey and pain points and creating a roadmap of questions and stages for your pipeline that can be measured, understood, and managed. But a good methodology, if it evolves, does more than that and it can help the sales team and the organization define who they are and what they want to do, and not do, as the company scales. A great methodology will help you get from whiteboard to PowerPoint to PDF, and that's the key to scaling.

13

Scaling the Operating System

Your operating system, like your methodology, will evolve over time as you scale. In the early stages you may find yourself doing far more than sales, and you may find yourself chasing a lot of things that don't play out, that take up a lot of time, and that leave you with little to show for your efforts. That's an artifact of being a startup, with all the unknowns. But as you generate some consistent revenues, as you build a methodology that can scale with you, you will be well-served by developing and abiding by an operating system.

In any sales organization, and especially if teams are distributed, it's critically important to create an environment that's safe for people, where they feel that they can be mentored and learn from each other. As the CRO, a 15-minute standup in the morning can be helpful in just getting everyone oriented to the day, it can help the team understand what's going on in the community, and it helps keep them accountable. As the leader, you would want to have one-to-one conversations once a week with each individual salesperson and ideally, a meeting once a week with the full team.

Meetings, if not managed properly, can quickly lose their value and it's the leader's responsibility to ensure that, if you're bringing everyone to a meeting once a week, there's value for the individuals and the company. No one gets value from a weekly meeting where each salesperson goes through their pipeline. We can read; we know what's in your pipeline. Tell us about the opportunities you have, the challenges you're facing, where you're stuck, what you've learned, what you heard about the competition. Talk about the dynamics of the business, both for the benefit of your team, and for the benefit of the CRO, as we all learn together about how our product is being received in-market.

That being said, it is critical to have weekly or bi-weekly pipeline and forecast reviews with your team, and then with management, that includes an assessment of "safe case" and "best case" scenarios for opportunities, so that you have visibility into the likely outcome for a month and/or quarter. This level of scrutiny improves discipline around pipeline management, and forecast integrity. It also is a tool that helps assess the relative performance of team members, and can offer coaching moments, especially if opportunities consistently "slip."

It's also important to have strategic meetings as well, at least quarterly. Thinking about the past quarter, what worked, what didn't? What would we do differently? What do we add, what do we subtract? And during the quarterly meeting we'd also roadmap for the next quarter. What are our goals? And how will we get there? Those kinds of questions are good to share to be sure that we're both tactically and strategically engaged as a means of being successful and as a means of learning from one another.

As the CRO, you want to create that fiber within the organization that connects the salespeople, so you want to bring everything from the outside in and bring everything inside to the salesperson. We would also encourage you to create as part of your operating system an invitation for others in the organization to interact with Sales. For example, You would want your Head of Product to know exactly what your prospects and customers are saying as a means of improvement and would invite that person to get on a sales call with someone from your team. That's an important part of both team engagement and engagement with the market.

The other component of an operating system that's important is performance management. It's a red flag if you have a sales organization that is consistently missing its numbers or is unable to deliver. You might not find out that you have a problem until you're six to nine months into a startup. But if you don't have a robust performance management program where you're very deliberate about the kind of coaching you need to get people up to performance, that is a potential hazard. You have to know, especially in a startup, both the speedway and the guardrails to get things going.

The specific performance management plan is obviously dependent on your sales cycle, and the time it takes to get from lead to close. Generally, it's good to give a rep one quarter to ramp, and begin to build pipeline. Assuming they get the training, coaching, and clear guidelines on the action needed to get to goal, you can begin monitoring performance on all aspects of selling, not just attainment. If a rep cannot get to 70% attainment for two quarters in a row, and they have received consistent feedback and support, an exit plan might be your best option. The rep should be aware of performance expectations at the outset, so that they can do what it takes to perform and succeed.

14

Marketing Alignment

No relationship for the CRO is more important than the one you have with the CMO. Marketing can help you get from the PowerPoint stage to the PDF stage, especially if Marketing has SDRs reporting to them and if Marketing is paying close attention to what works. If you're a CRO without a very good personal and professional relationship with your CMO, you're setting yourself up for failure. Notice that we didn't say, a very good professional relationship only, but a personal relationship, too. That's important, especially as you're scaling because there will be mistakes, miscues, miscommunication, and a host of other issues that strain a professional relationship, but a personal relationship can overcome these. But developing a strong relationship with Marketing is critical in getting to the PDF stage for the sales organization.

If you're new to the CRO role, or if you're starting with a new company as a CRO, your first order of business is to develop a relationship of mutual respect and understanding with the Head of Marketing, and together develop a commitment for Sales and Marketing to work together. If you don't do that, you'll have problems scaling. For example, at Return Path we missed our quarter, missed our targets and goals, which is a yellow flag. And then Marketing stood up and said everything's green—we made our goals, we made our quarter. That's a problem! If Sales is yellow and Marketing is green, that's a huge indicator that there's misalignment because Marketing and Sales should be tied to revenue. After providing that feedback, however, we never had that issue again.

The CRO and Head of Marketing need to make sure there's alignment around goals and objectives, around messaging and positioning, around a concept of continuous improvement and experimentation. The level of visibility, interaction, and alignment around positioning messaging, strategy is critical. Beyond that, Sales and Marketing need alignment around shared goals and objectives.

One of the best ways to strengthen the relationship between Sales and Marketing, to accelerate that alignment, is through structure. You do this by having the SDR and inside sales report to Marketing and by doing that you'll have shared goals and objectives for both the pipeline and lead generation. We had this structure at Return Path and Voxy, where the inside Sales team reported to Marketing so that Marketing deeply shared our pipeline creation goals. After all, Marketing manages the team that delivered potentially half of the pipeline.

Not only were we aligned on the pipeline, but also we were aligned in our go-to-market messaging. Our outbound campaigns to support the Sales team had to be completely aligned with Marketing; they had to direct their marketing machine to build the pipeline. It's also helpful that the CRO look for opportunities to bring Marketing into the sales process. You can listen in and participate on sales calls, or staff the booth at a conference or trade show along with your sales team. That way you're learning from one another and creating content that can be used for webinars, blog posts, LinkedIn posts, or any other social media. Through these opportunities you'll build the market knowledge so that Marketing deeply understands the market, from both a Sales and a Marketing perspective.

There are several different ways to structure the role of the SDR, based in part on how your company is structured regionally, and also personal preference. One way is to have the SDRs support all of the salespeople. If you have a weak performer, a single sales rep is not saddled with that person and if you have a strong performer, that talent will be distributed more broadly to all the sales reps. The SDRs can be compensated for both the number of meetings and percentage of opportunities that close. You want the SDRs to have the opportunity to benefit from working with a variety of salespeople and you want the SDRs to learn about Sales, so that they can understand possible career paths for themselves. Other CROs take a SWAT team approach, but an environment where we can learn from shared best practices, as opposed to creating little silos is more effective. If you manage the sales organization in secret, without full candor (like what happens when things are in silos), then it has the potential for problems.

Although Marketing and Sales each have their individual goals, they also have shared goals around pipeline creation, around lead generation, and by having SDRs report to Marketing, those shared objectives keep them on the same page. It enables you to celebrate successes and to learn from one another's misfires, campaigns that didn't work, or messaging that didn't work. Having that openness and communication and shared goals helps you get to the point where you can collaborate for the most impact and success. And that collaboration is fundamental to being able to scale.

What I Look for in a Startup Chief Revenue Officer/Head of Sales

About once a week I hear an entrepreneur during a financing presentation tell me that the product is "almost ready" for general availability. They'll follow that up with, "Now all we need to do is hire a VP of Sales." I typically respond by asking them some tough, pointed questions about their sales process because usually entrepreneurs at this early stage haven't had enough repetitions to truly understand the ideal customer journey and making it result in sales. Hiring a VP of Sales at this time would not be the right person to hire first, because you don't want to scale up a process you don't truly understand yet. It would be a grave and costly mistake for the entrepreneur and for the person hired.

So, who should startups hire first? Sadly, there is no one answer other than "it depends." It depends on the stage of the company and the maturity of the process. The key thing in the first phase is to figure that out. The simple truth is that most startups at the early stages do not need a highly experienced sales leader. The first "sales team" is founder-led by the person who brings a deep knowledge of the product to market, who has the impressive title of founder/CEO, and hopefully, who has the charisma to help people overcome their reluctance to buy something new.

At some point, the CEO needs to build a sales team, and the temptation is to hire a VP of Sales first. I've rarely seen this work. A more proven approach is to hire a smart, hungry sales apprentice. Former CEO of MobileIron, Bob Tinker, refers to this person as a Davy Crockett, "someone who can find the path through the woods." The job at this point is not merely to go out and try to find revenue, but to help develop a process that can be replicated in the future. To do that, the first sales hire has to be smart, creative, and aggressive. They need to have more ability than traditional reps to understand the product and where it fits, to find new use cases, to invent new paths into the market. And they need to be strategic enough to learn from the experiments and figure out what is potentially repeatable. Your first sales hire doesn't need to be particularly senior; in fact, a senior leader isn't usually hungry enough to get this job done.

Once the sale process is more defined, which often means you've got a couple of "Davy Crocketts" out selling, *then* you need a VP of Sales. This person needs the leadership and judgment to hire and build a team (including figuring out the right rep profile), the decisiveness to lay out a basic framework (quotas, territory assignment, mix of SDRs, reps, and systems engineers, early sales training), and the adaptability to step in and change when one part of the formula isn't working well enough. And at this stage, the company still requires someone who is willing to be out in the field, working deals with reps to close the quarter successfully.

When the company is ready to step on the gas and scale, you'll need to hire a Chief Revenue Officer (CRO). For a SaaS company, this is typically at $15–20m in ARR, more than 15 sales reps, and a fairly repeatable sales process. At this point, the leader needs to be a systems thinker, a process builder, and a planner. This job is really more like a field general in command of significant resources that need to be positioned and coordinated to achieve scale and efficiency. They need to have the judgment to hire good managers and the sales capacity to close the best ones, the ability to work together with the rest of the executive team, and they need to know how much process is appropriate for the current scale of the company. As the company is ready to add new geographies (e.g., EMEA, APAC) or new channels and partners, the CRO should have the experience, judgment, and network to be able to initiate those efforts with a strong initial plan and team.

But there is much more that is highly variable depending upon the stage of the company and, even more importantly, its sales maturity. As above, the answer to what you need in a CRO/VP of Sales/first sales hire is, "It depends." But hopefully, I've given you some ideas about "on what exactly, does it depend?" and how to determine what the right role scope and the right capabilities are for your company right now. **Greg Sands, *Founder, Managing Director at Costanoa Ventures***

15

Market Assessment and Alignment

As you're scaling, you should have a lot of enthusiasm around a new product, around the market you want to penetrate, and around the new business that you'll generate. But that enthusiasm can also be a trap unless you are able to be honest about your prospects. We don't mean your prospects as potential customers, but your prospects in the market. A framework of "What must be true?" is a good way to assess new markets, it is a helpful framework to understand if you can expand and move to adjacent markets.

Being truly honest in determining and understanding the factors that could potentially affect your growth is a necessary first step and you should be rigorous (and conservative) about answering questions like the total addressable market and other areas. For example, what privacy or legal restrictions may you have, or may you face that you haven't initially anticipated? What does the competitive landscape look like? Do you have an upstart competitor that potentially sees opportunity and is willing to disrupt? Have there been any factors that affected the overall vitality of your offering and that might impact your pricing? Is this sale repeatable enough to a large enough market that we can move to selling with PDF, or are we forever going to be stuck at the PowerPoint stage?

Scaling involves reevaluating the factors that made you successful as a startup and you need to revisit those factors to be sure that you can expand either the distribution channels or geographies. If you just go in blindly without being very conscious of what factors must be true for you to be successful, you have the potential to trip up and either miss additional opportunity or over-estimate what your real total addressable market (TAM) and opportunity are or create an organizational mess in pursuit of growth.

It is important to note that not all growth has to be organic. At Return Path, we made several critical acquisitions in the early days (Delivery Assurance Systems and Bonded Sender), that gave us the product and technology platforms that helped us grow and scale the business. That was incredibly positive.

However, somewhere between $50–75m in revenue, we began to understand that our target market wasn't large enough to support the kind of long-term growth we'd need to go public, one of our goals at the time. So, we thought about adjacent spaces we could potentially step into leveraging our core assets to try to expand our reach. And that decision, to expand our reach, led to all sorts of ideas and experiments and new products. That expansion led Scott Weiss, one of our independent Board members, to comment that we had become "the world's smallest conglomerate." We ended up with disparate businesses that had slightly different audiences with slightly different market messages with slightly different product requirements. The resources we needed to keep all of those going was a real drain on the organization. We ended up selling off all of those businesses.

Even Slight Misalignment can Cause Problems

> I ran one of those businesses, Consumer Insight, for Return Path at the end of my tenure there. It was a great, great idea because we could use the same data we were using for our core business and repurpose it for a different customer segment. The problem was we could never invest enough to truly leverage the opportunity across the Return Path customer base. We isolated and identified that market research companies and hedge funds had the sophistication and the appetite to collect these huge data feeds, so we chased them. But once we got past the low hanging fruit of the 10 market research companies and the 25 hedge funds who could use this data, where are you? The investment to make our data truly consumable, and packaged for a broader customer base of mainstream was beyond our means. **Anita Absey**

We didn't waste time and money (we sold the business), but we had engineering resources that arguably could have been deployed elsewhere to improve other products. If you're going to chase an opportunity, if you're thinking of expanding to adjacent markets, make sure that you're really honest about what the actual potential is with what you have today. The best way to begin that exercise is to create a list of answers to the question, "What must be true?"

16

Expanding Distribution Channels

Our experience has been primarily in B2B businesses and in other companies it will differ, but in our experience when you're starting out, you start out as a direct seller. As a direct seller, you really understand the dynamics of the market, what resonates with customers, and you create your own positioning, messaging, branding, pricing, and packaging, that gives you a very refined and comprehensive understanding of what's important in order to be successful in selling.

Soon thereafter, it's really important if you want to expand the reach of your message to align with partners, to expand and develop your channel. By aligning with the right partners for your product, you'll amplify your partner's products, helping them sell more or helping them reduce customer churn. Channel business is not really about generating revenues for the partner from your product—it's great if it happens—but the real advantages are that you get access to a channel for your product that you wouldn't otherwise have, and you're helping someone else be successful.

If you can find partners where your product is additive to theirs, they'll be highly motivated to work with you. The incentive can't just be to sell more of your product, it has to be making their business better. If you can find those partners, I've seen it be incredibly successful, but not without conflict.

Finding the Right Channel Partner

At Voxy, I had a small direct sales team of about 10 people but we could never hire fast enough to be able to materially grow our business. I introduced the concept of trying to work with channel partners and although they resisted in the beginning, we eventually got it working. The company's product was a technology platform that helps people around the world learn how to speak English. The companies we partnered with were ones where our technology enabled them to provide more value to their customers.

For instance, we partnered with employment agencies, who have huge numbers of people that they need to fill all kinds of roles and they need that employee population to learn how to speak English. By offering our solution to their employers, it was able to help its employee population speak English, so that was tremendously valuable to them.

Another channel included nonprofits who had as their mission educating a refugee population. A nonprofit like the Red Cross could see how providing our product as part of their suite that they were giving to their populations, employees or otherwise, would be enhanced. Within two years we went from zero and increased our sales by 20% in channel business, which is a big leap when you're a startup. **Anita Absey**

The right channel partner helps get leverage in the market and also helps you take advantage of branding with well-known companies. You may never have heard of Voxy, but you probably have heard of the Red Cross, of UNICEF, or other refugee agencies. For a small company looking to expand, a channel partner can give your brand cachet whether it's private labeled, or whether it's something that's powered by your brand. But it's a critically important growth strategy.

You may run into resistance with your CEO or CFO in approaching a channel partner like the ones mentioned above, and one way to couch it with a CFO or even a CEO is to acknowledge that this is a lower margin sales strategy but the top line growth should far exceed the worry about the margin. And that has typically proven itself to be the case with regards to brand value. And your brand value can add cachet to your partner. Our company was very contemporary and innovative in the English language learning space, so in some cases the brand was the cachet and our partners could say, "powered by ...," signaling that they were working with a top company in the space. Others preferred their own brand, which is fine.

The channel strategy we're advocating is not without work on the CRO's part. It's not the case that you can find a partner where your product is additive to theirs and then sit back and ship out orders. You'll have to work with the partner marketing team, helping them bring your product to market, establishing messaging and potentially marketing through them so that you can offer webinars and conferences that help educate their customer population.

It also helps to have a person or team that manages channel partners and is responsible for training the partner and making sure they're fluent in your product. Your team should also provide partner support and traditional customer service. But the partner should be responsible for delivering service and value to their customers.

One important note: this is not easy. There will be inevitable conflict between your channel and direct teams, unless you can establish clear rules of engagement (always lean into the partner), and commission that rewards both channel and direct teams in the event of conflict. This will promote trust with the partner, and encourage your direct rep to take the commission and move on to close more deals in their territory. You do have to be sure that your direct reps remain productive, and do not only benefit from deals sold through a partner.

Expanding your reach through channel partners is a lower margin business and if you have a really aggressive partner, they can take up to 50% of the bookings for themselves. But if they're marketing and they're servicing and they're selling, that's a good outcome as long as the top line growth justifies giving up that much margin.

17

Geographic Expansion

When you're ready for geographic expansion, you'll use the market assessment framework you've already created for scaling up. The litmus test that you have to pass to know whether you're ready to expand to new geographies starts with a list of answers to the question, "What must be true?" What must be true for you to be successful globally?

With Voxy, the English language learning software, our first "What must be true?" was that the government had to support that their constituents learn English. Without that driver, it would not make sense to expand to a new geography. Similarly, with LRN, the ethics and compliance software company, our "What must be true?" was that ethics and compliance training had to be mandated by the U.S. Department of Justice, or by the zeal of companies to protect corporate brands.

There won't be just one "What has to be true?" factor, but many factors that you'll want to consider to be successful in a particular region. If you have a list of ten factors, they don't all have to be weighted equally and there might be five things that would be sufficient to get you to 85% of where you need to be. You'll have to experiment to be sure that you're not letting great be the enemy of very good. Nothing is going to be perfect at any given time so you'll have to be sensible about how you weigh and prioritize what must be true to be successful.

Some countries seem like ripe opportunities, just given their population, but you'll have to dig deeper to understand whether your business can take hold there. For instance, in China, it's very difficult to do business because there are so many entrenched competitors. Let that be your guide as well. People said to us at Voxy, "China's the largest population in the world demanding to speak English, why don't you expand there?" But our competitors had hundreds of people on the ground and we were just a 75-person company. Despite the huge demand and appetite to learn English, and despite our superior software, it didn't make sense. But Vietnam was attractive, so we went there.

The long and short of it is that you'll need to be honest with yourself about what must be true for your product and what must be true for your company to adapt and fit into a new culture with all that it entails. In most countries you'll need to have native people as part of your team to really be successful. Even if you get some inbound leads from regions you hadn't expected, you still need to be much more deliberate and collaborative with the executive team to expand globally. Because a lot must be true.

Some Geographies are Just...Difficult

When contemplating geographic expansion, you cannot just chase dollars without understanding the complexities of entering a market, doing business locally, and accurately assessing overall market potential. There are some geographies that are just difficult, regardless of what you think the upside is, and even if your "What must be true?" is true. We succumbed to this temptation at Return Path as we started responding to inquiries to sell our solutions into Russia. We spent too much time and travel trying to wrangle opportunities, only to realize that we were deluded by the prospect of success, without truly understanding the long-term viability of the market. It ended up being a waste of our energy, time, and resources. **Anita Absey**

Your decision to expand cannot be at the behest of a lone wolf salesperson saying, "Hey, I can close this big deal in China." You need to have the people in the home office ready and able to support global expansion enthusiastically and embrace a total growth strategy. Otherwise, if you try to go it alone with your sales organization, you'll do it in fits and starts and you likely won't have the kind of resources you need to nurture and grow business outside of the United States. You'll have to market in a new environment, hire local people to sell the product and provide service, you'll need to have commitments from the product team because they may need to adjust your solution based on local needs.

As you're figuring out your business model and as you're seeing that you will be able to scale successfully, then you should absolutely be thinking about international expansion. In many of the companies I've worked at, international business accounted for 50% of our bookings. But you'll need to be nimble and flexible and it's critical that you do it in a way that's scalable and repeatable. You'll need the back office and framework for getting business done to be nailed down, noting that there may be little nuances to pay attention to that will help you be more successful.

18

Pricing and Packaging

Pricing

Pricing and packaging are two areas where many startups trip up, either because they don't do discovery well in the beginning or they don't understand the competitive landscape. If you're selling into an existing market but maybe you have a new mousetrap, you've got a slicker product and more innovation, or deliver the solution or the technology faster, the best approach is to price the way people buy it. Don't try to break the model. If it's a per seat model, then don't try to change that structure, try to fit within it so that you're competitively priced. Unless you can deliver materially more value that enables you to get a higher price, then your best strategy is to be competitively priced.

It's always a matter of testing and having a working theory of what can work so that you're not just going in asking someone, "Well, what would you pay for this?" Because their response is likely to be, "Well, you know what, I'm going to give you a low price of what I would pay for it." But if you can create scenarios that help someone understand how the value and price equation works, then you have something that they can hold on to and you can help them understand as you're pricing, what value you're delivering at the same time.

If you're going to a brand new space, then it might require a little bit more experimentation to determine pricing. The strategy here is to align your pricing model with how the customer uses your product. If they use your product for every mail campaign they send out, for example, then you might want to charge by campaigns, and not by number of emails. But it's important to understand the cost structure that your customer has and what value they get from your product, what revenue they're collecting, so that you fit into that in a meaningful way and that your price point is not so high. It's very much experimentation when you're in a brand new market but with some working theories you can begin to discover, hopefully not through trial and error but through experimentation, what works. This approach is particularly helpful in the beginning, before you've scaled.

As you scale, price becomes incredibly important. I am viscerally opposed to discounting as a means of getting business. If you're priced too high and you keep losing deals based on that, then contemplate changing your pricing structure or creating a lower-end offering that is differentiated from the full price offering. But if you discount just to get business, you're demeaning the value of what you bring to the market. And this is even more true as you expand in the market because you need to understand what the market will bear, not how low you can price your product. Finally, this will be incredibly disruptive to your business in markets where customers talk to one another. Being as consistent as possible with pricing, and pricing practices, will help you maintain the price/value ratio in market.

In scaling up, your competitive intelligence is paramount and you'll have to constantly be looking around to see what the competition is doing. Ask yourself, is there a way I can do this more simply? Is there an easier way for a prospect to work with me and a customer to sign a contract? That doesn't necessarily mean you have to undo what you've done from the beginning, but you have to constantly be wary of changes in the market, you have to know how budgets may be impacted at your customer that could potentially affect how you price and how you package your product.

Packaging

In terms of packaging, there are several ways to think about it. Some companies like to do the menu approach where every single thing has a price. When you do that, you may be giving the impression that you're nickel and diming somebody. The opposite of that is bundling things together, like when the cable company offers "packages," and whether or not you want something, you have to pay for it. There's got to be a balance between those two, but in packaging your product, it's best to listen to your prospect, listen to your customer. Just because something is bright and shiny to you as the seller may not actually be important to the buyer. For example, many people would be so much happier with their cable company if they didn't make them pay for a local sports channel, if they never use it. Even if it's $1 a month, it's just irritating and customers will feel as if they are being taken advantage of. But if you can be sensitive to what's important to your customer and prospect and you include their ideas, you'll have a better sense on how to package things.

But try not to provide a laundry list of pricing that you share with them because that is not a good customer experience and you should try to offer a holistic bundle of services or products that make most sense to your buyer.

Regardless of what you want to do, you may have to match the market you're in. In B2B and SaaS companies there's a fee structure based on the number of users. That's a seat model and it's very common.

But one thing you can control on pricing is how much flexibility you give to your salespeople, and a good approach is to give them a lot of flexibility within ranges that you define. If a salesperson wants to discount by 10%, that's fine if that's within your realm because some customers always want a discount. But if it's more than that, maybe you want to have a more stringent set of internal approvals. Also, when we say that it's fine for a salesperson to offer a discount, we don't want them to discount on the last day of the quarter just to hit their quota. That type of discounting diminishes you as a brand, as a company, and as a provider. You would be better off walking away than cut prices by 30% to close a deal.

Of course, we understand that the market is viciously competitive, and oftentimes you do have to use price as a means of leverage, it's just not the preferred way to operate in the market. The preferred way is to focus on the concept of value and impact and outcomes, and to really paint a picture for the prospect on how you can help their business. And then that value price equation is much easier to accept and agree on.

It's also true that salespeople are often met, invariably up front, with the question, "What's your price?" That question often comes early in the sales process, before you've had a chance to discover the needs and problems of the customer and before you've had a chance to ask questions and demonstrate value. In this case, the response is, "I'm happy to give you a price. In return, I need to get some information from you. I need to be able to ask you questions so that I can give you a range of what's relevant."

Similarly, if you're asked for a proposal early in the selling process, then the response is always, "Yes, but in return I'd like to get a meeting with the key buyers to understand your decision process or understand your issues better." That's a very common response to a question that comes very early in the process, typically by customers who are very price-conscious. It's not a deal breaker, but you should work to get something in return for your efforts. It's a give and get strategy, very simple but important.

As you scale, pricing is critically important and the process of discovering your pricing and packaging is very much that: a process of discovery.

The Wisdom of Anita

> I had the pleasure of working with Anita as a leader in Sales, Service, Customer Success, Marketing, and GM for almost two decades. Over that time, I gained so much from Anita's experience—but even more from her ability to concisely wrap up thoughts into a key phrase. Here are a few of Anita's greatest hits:

- **God gave you two ears and one mouth for a reason.** It's so important to listen to your customers in sales pitches instead of just running through your pitch deck and spouting out features and benefits.

- **Hope is not a strategy.** Too many sales leaders throw "Hail Mary" passes at the end of too many quarters. If you're methodical about sales math and understand your conversion metrics and work collaboratively to make your sales funnel and sales power line up, you'll hit your numbers more times than not.

- **Feedback is a gift, whether you want it or not.** Brilliant advice for anyone looking to improve in sales, or looking to advance their career from sales, into sales management, ultimately into sales leadership.

- **You can't fall off the floor.** Taking on a new sales management challenge, whether you're doing so at a fresh startup or in a scaleup looking to improve its sales leadership, or in a turnaround situation, is always easiest when you remember that sometimes, you can only improve on what's gone before you.

- **We need to go to the gym on that.** Sales training is not a three-hour seminar you attend once. It's something you need to work on every single day with your manager or sales trainer. When you've mastered one technique, there's another one to move onto.

- **May all your months have 35 days.** For any sales department ever ... enough said! **Matt Blumberg,** *Executive Chair, Bolster*

III. CRO AND THE LEADERSHIP TEAM

19

How to Hire a Chief Revenue Officer

Anita Absey

Earlier, in Chapter 6 (Profile of Successful Salespeople), I highlighted that the qualities you'd want to look for in a sales representative include excellent communication and listening skills, self-motivation, and a passion for the chase and win. I also mentioned that in a leader you would want all of those qualities plus a person who excels at hiring, coaching and mentoring, a person who embodies the vision and mission of the organization, and who will set the tone and tenor to inspire performance and accountability across the sales organization. When it comes to the CRO, of course you would expect all of those qualities plus the gravitas to work effectively with other C-suite executives, board members, and executives at clients. But before you charge ahead and bring in a CRO to your startup or scaleup, I find that it's helpful to understand that the impact of a CRO is partly dependent on their skills, but also dependent on your company and how you operate.

Given the wide range of paths that people take to get to the CRO level it can be daunting to figure out the best person to lead your sales organization. To help you think through the hiring of a CRO I use the concept of *personas* as a framework to identify the people who will excel in a particular company, and those who, despite stellar skills and credentials, will struggle. I have found that there are four distinct *personas* that define the vast majority of sales leaders—field sales, inside sales, channel sales, and full stack—and they are relatively distinct and cohesive so that people in one *persona* will be similar to all others in that *persona* but different from people in the other *personas*. By the time you get to the CRO level, you are obviously familiar with different types of sales organizations but each person will have preferences, values, and deeper experience in one *persona* rather than deep experience in all of them. Choosing the right CRO for your startup depends on finding a person with the *persona* that will make a big impact in your company moving forward. So, if you're a B2C startup, someone within the channel *persona* might be a better choice than someone who has experience in B2B and field sales.

Persona Attributes and How to Find Them

A person within the field sales *persona* is someone who is skilled in taking leads and closing them in person and while that may sound simple, a field sales organization is often used by businesses that sell products at high price points. When you are selling products above $100k, the stakes are often high, the sales process is often long, and because it's a big decision for the customer, direct personal interaction is often required. Not every salesperson is capable of closing large deals, even if they are warm leads, but a field salesperson who can think strategically and engage tactically will excel in these challenging situations. On LinkedIn or other platforms, look for people who have an entrepreneurial spirit or have been entrepreneurs themselves. Perhaps they have had success in scaling businesses, or have a track record of meeting revenue targets and growing and building teams. People with the ability to work at high levels in customer organizations are rare but if you need to sell at high prices and you are selling to sophisticated customers, a field sales *persona* might be your best option.

A second *persona* common in sales organizations is what is referred to as inside sales, although terms like remote sales, virtual sales, or high velocity sales are also commonly used. A person within the inside sales *persona* will generally make sales over the phone and while sales of this type are lower touch, for the companies that need inside sales a CRO with those skills is invaluable. Many companies that sell products with short sales cycles and lower price points will use inside sales and even companies with high price points will use inside sales teams to generate leads for field salespeople to close in larger enterprise organizations. An inside sales *persona* will be able to manage the talent conveyer belt, manage metrics and use CRM particularly well. It's relatively straightforward to find people with inside sales experience on LinkedIn or other platforms because they will have experience as an SDR, experience qualifying inbound and creating outbound leads and they will understand the metrics associated with running a successful inside sales organization. You should expect them to have a proven record of success and be able to develop sales playbooks.

The channel sales *persona* is typical of companies that sell products through a third-party distributor to the end consumer. For example, if you purchase a new computer you might find a security package like Norton on your Dell computer or, at Bolster, we have a number of IT products being sold to Bolster by US Computer. A channel sales *persona* will work with their partners / distributors to ensure that they are up to date on their company's newest products and well trained and incentivized to sell them. The channel partner must also be able to understand why your product enhances their ability to sell and retain customers. Channel sales are most often used by companies at a large scale, but can also be leveraged by smaller companies without an established brand, to get a foothold in the market. On LinkedIn or another platform, a channel sales *persona* will most likely have experience selling other companies products as a sales representative, or has run a channel business from scratch as a means to grow and scale a startup. Although inside sales and field sales are relatively close in terms of the selling process, they are quite different from the channel sales process and if you choose a field sales CRO, for example, and you mostly have channel sales, that person will have to work to ensure that the direct and channel teams have a symbiotic relationship because that is critical to the success of both teams.

A full stack *persona* is a person who owns all of the revenue generating functions in a company and would likely have oversight over channels, inside sales and field sales. It is also common for the full stack *persona* to have revenue operations, sales enablement and sometimes marketing reporting into this role. This role is relevant in later stage companies and companies that may want to expand globally. On LinkedIn or another platform you'll be able to find the full stack CRO by looking for a person with prior experience as a CRO in a company that has successfully scaled from a startup to high growth. Absent that CRO title, a person who has managed multiple teams and functions, understands the deep connections needed among all company departments in enabling sales team success, or has been a leader of a sales function, may be ready for a CRO role.

When Is The Right Time For This *Persona*?

You may look over the four *personas* and conclude that the full stack *persona* is the best candidate for the CRO role. After all, the full stack CRO has experience as a CRO, has successfully scaled a startup to high growth, and has experience as the leader of multiple functions reporting into them. But recall the advice (Chapter 13) from Greg Sands: Most startups in early stages do not need a fully-fledged CRO, and what they really need is a Head of Sales, a VP of Sales—someone who understands the market of the startup where it is now, not where it wants to be. If you hire a CRO before you have enough repetitions to understand the customer journey, not only will the CRO fail, but your company could fail, too. If you are still at the whiteboard stage you are still experimenting, you are still figuring out the most basic aspects of your GTM. Even being at the PowerPoint stage may be too early to hire a CRO because there are still unanswered questions and you won't be able to scale, no matter how talented your CRO hire is. You must be at the PDF stage to have any hope of hiring a CRO who can make an impact.

You Don't Need a CRO

One of the most common things early-stage CEOs say to me once they find product-market fit and make a few sales is, "I need a CRO." The answer is almost always, "No, you don't."

In the early days of a company, it's all "selling on whiteboard." The need that early-stage CEOs have that prompts them to tell me they need a CRO is simple: they need to have help selling.

But what the CEO really needs is a couple of very good early-stage sales reps. They need people who are senior enough and clever enough to hold clients' attention, yet who are also junior enough to accompany the CEO or other founders on dozens of "selling on whiteboard" sessions with clients to be able to start doing that work on their own. And they need people who can help make the transition from "selling on whiteboard" to "selling on Powerpoint" by doing some very basic documentation of the selling process, buying centers, influencers, and value proposition.

It may also be true that the CEO doesn't really know much about sales — maybe it's a technical founder, or even a founder who came up through marketing or product management — and that part of the "I need a CRO" comment is really just an admission that the CEO doesn't really know how to structure and manage a sales effort. In that case, consider the over 1,200 fractional CROs in the Bolster Network who can give you anything from an hour of consulting to a couple days per week as a fractional executive to help you put some structure in place for your new sales reps. Once you have a repeatable sales motion, you can hire more reps and a Sales Manager/Director or VP.

So no, you don't need a CRO. But there are lots of things you can do to get the help you need in the early days of selling that are less expensive, less risky, and a better fit for early-stage companies.

Matt Blumberg, *Executive Chair, Bolster*

https://startupceo.com/2023/10/you-dont-need-a-cro

But, what do you do if you're not at the PDF stage but you need to create a sales organization? Here I would suggest that you hire a VP that fits the *persona* that is right for your company. For example, you can hire a VP Field Sales in the early stages, and this person must have the gravitas to get meetings with senior level people or execs, and still be able to do the direct selling, initially. Once product/market fit, pricing, and competition are understood, then this person can hire a team of sellers. And with experience, this person could become your CRO.

If your startup requires inside sales then once you have found product/market fit and once you understand what it takes to grow the business, then you could hire a VP Inside sales. That is also when you could hire several sales development reps (SDRs). The SDRs would be responsible for qualifying inbound leads and sourcing outbound leads. The VP Inside Sales needs to have very close alignment with Marketing, and experience in creating campaigns and sequences to attract potential buyers. So, in addition to deep experience in inside sales, your VP should also be a strong collaborator, not a lone wolf.

You can hire a VP of channel sales when you have product / market fit, when you have your pricing figured out, and when your competitive and market dynamics are well understood. Finally, when a company is $15MM+ in ARR, that is the time to consider the full stack CRO. If you are contemplating hiring more regional managers, and you are potentially expanding globally, that is the time to hire a full stack CRO. This person will need to have the wherewithal to ensure that a solid, common language exists in understanding the problems the company solves; they will have to collaborate with the CMO with an eye toward instituting scalable and repeatable business processes; and they will need to collaborate with the CCO to understand the customer engagement and retention dynamics to be sure that the sales organization is bringing on the right customers.

General Interview Questions

Although I have identified four *personas* in sales that ought to serve you well in hiring your first (or next) CRO, there are some general questions you can ask each CRO candidate.

- What was your mandate when you joined the business? Where are your fingerprints?

- How has your role evolved over your time there?

- How big is the business today? (revenue and people)

- What did your team look like? Do you hire the team or inherit, or mix of both?

- When you joined___, what was in place? Did you have to build a sales process, playbook, implement salesforce?

- Do you own all of the company's revenue streams? ...which don't you own?

- Who do you report to?

- What percentage of revenue does your team account for? How has that grown YOY?

- Where is revenue today? What is the size of the sales team today?

- What's the most complex value proposition you've had to sell? (looking for solutions into companies, not products into divisions)

- Who do you sell into?

  - Types of companies i.e. Enterprise/Midmarket/SMB

  - Level of person they're selling to (CTO, CMO, Ad planners, account team, etc.)

- Do you still carry a bag?

- What's the average sales cycle?

- What's the ASP?

Questions For Each *Persona*

There are also questions you would want to ask of each *persona*. For a field sales candidate you can ask, "What specific experience do you have in making revenue targets, building teams, and scaling a business.?" I would ask for detailed examples and you ought to expect that your candidate will be able to easily and comfortably provide details on how they have accomplished these things, what they have done, and what lessons they have learned that would be relevant to the CRO role. I would also probe whether the candidate has experience developing sales playbooks and has done territory and account planning because those are important in developing your sales operating system.

Another question to ask a field sales candidate is, "Please give me some examples of where you have failed, and the lessons you learned from that experience, and how you changed your behavior." Here I would be looking for candor and authenticity. If someone cannot give an example of where they have failed, and what they have learned, that is a red flag. And finally, I would ask, "What do you think are the most important attributes in a successful salesperson? A successful sales leader?" My expectation (hope!) is that a candidate will respond that empathy, listening skills, eagerness to help people solve business problems, and a zeal to combine these attributes for success define a good salesperson and also define a good sales leader. In addition, a sales leader must have the ability to coach and mentor the salesperson, and not do the job for them. I would also expect an answer that a good salesperson and good sales leader will have a deep understanding of the product feature/function/advantage/benefit, as well as an understanding of the market. Those are just table stakes but it's important for the CRO candidate to articulate them.

For an inside sales candidate I would ask, "Can you share with me some examples of SDR campaigns that you have conducted successfully as a rep? Are there some examples that you did not execute well? What have you learned from the successful and unsuccessful campaigns?" I would expect a deep understanding of the mechanics of a successful SDR campaign, and what works and what does not work. Another question to ask the inside sales candidate is, "Typically, an SDR is early in their sales career and it is often their first job. How do you manage new talent to the business? What type of skills do you look for, and what kind of training do you provide?" Here I would look for someone who understands how critical it is to manage someone at the early stages of their career. I would also look for answers that highlight a candidate's willingness and experience in coaching and training people early in their career to success, rather than to an exit out of the company.

Finally, a good question to ask the inside sales candidate is, "What metrics do you use to manage the success of the team? How visible is this to the team and the organization?" And the reason to ask that question is that inside sales is a numbers game, with a well-worn process of templates, sequences, and communication channels to utilize. I would expect an inside sales candidate to provide insight and deep knowledge into what it takes to be successful...including number of calls, emails, timing, and other important metrics.

For the channel sales candidate I would ask, "What do you think are the most important things to consider when growing and scaling a channel business?" I would expect to hear them articulate a response about how any channel partnership will help the partner grow and scale their business and retain customers. I also want to hear about flexibility, about willingness to modify positioning to suit the partner's needs. If the answer is just that we can provide the partner more revenue, that is too shallow an approach.

Another question to ask is, "How do you collaborate with the Partner's selling team and the direct sales team in your organization? What types of ongoing dialog and interaction do you have?" I am looking for an understanding of what it takes to be relevant to the Partner's sales team, and I would expect the candidate to provide some examples of ongoing engagement, some training, and potentially incentives. I also want to be sure that the candidate understands the inherent potential conflict between the direct and channel teams internally, and has ideas on how to mitigate that.

Finally, I would ask the channel sales candidate, "How do you bring on new Partners without alienating existing partners?" This is a tough question to answer and requires some thought and nuance. If you are the industry standard then you can engage with multiple partners and be sure the partners understand that their ability to succeed depends on their unique attributes. and your product/service is an enhancement. But if you are not the industry standard then your answer to the question has to be more creative and more sensitive to the situation you are in.

For the full stack candidate I would ask, "Provide detailed examples of how you have led the sales organization and include in these examples both successes and failures." I want to be sure this person is naturally fluent in what it takes to be a CRO, and how they translate their vision and the vision of the company into practical sales tactics. I also want to understand the experience this person has had in scaling high growth companies, and what pitfalls to avoid. Some pitfalls you might hear, or you should expect to hear, are that not every customer is a good customer or, do not let the zeal for making the numbers cloud good business judgement. They don't have to be these specific pitfalls, but the full stack candidate ought to have the experience and perspective to have learned something about a good sales organization.

Another question to ask the full stack candidate is, "Describe their management style." Ideally, their management style is based on what their direct reports need, not so much on what they think is the best management style. I personally would not want a micro-manager but there are situations that call for a very hand's-on style. A more thoughtful approach that can get the same result as micromanaging is through coaching and mentoring technique, and you may hear responses from the full stack candidate that echo this approach.

Finally, for the full stack candidate a question they ought to expect is, "What are the most important factors in running a successful sales organization?" Nearly every candidate should expect this question, or a variation of it, and I would hope that a candidate would state things like continuous learning and education from and with one another on the team, or failing fast and learning from mistakes, or creating a culture of accountability and performance, but not a competitive boiler room culture. You might also hear answers involving metrics to understand and manage the business, which are certainly a hallmark of a good sales organization.

Although there are a number of questions beyond the one listed here, finding the right CRO involves understanding your company well, understanding the markets in which you compete, the customers you sell to, and understanding the *persona* that best matches the impact you hope to make. Regardless of which *persona* fits your situation, you can still insist that your CRO hire establish a culture of accountability and performance, and you can hope that your new hire will create the fiber that connects salespeople to customers and to multiple stakeholders within the company.

20

How I Work With the Leadership Team

Anita Absey

When you become a CRO you will be working closely with the leadership team and to do that well it requires that you and others create a working relationship of candor, trust, openness, collaboration, and mutual respect for one another's roles. My experience on how to work well with the leadership team is based on both working very successfully with other executives and having been involved in very unfortunate experiences, too. It is easy, as a member of the leadership team, to want to promote your part of the business but it can be disastrous if you think that your part of the business is the most important part of the company. For example, if an engineering leader thinks that they are carrying the weight of the company because everything depends on them for new product creation, then that is not actually giving consideration or respect for what the marketing team has to do to promote the product or what the sales leadership team has to do to get products into the hands of prospects and customers.

At Return Path Matt did a very good job of forging positive bonds and relationships among the executive team and that took primacy over everything else. If there was a problematic relationship or something didn't work out, he would remove that person from the role because he didn't want to disrupt the harmony of that team to get things done. That's a best-case scenario of how a leadership team can be effective, but I have also seen worst case scenarios. In one company I worked at the executive team was completely out of sync and nothing got done. The sales numbers were off, customer retention was bad, product development was off base, marketing was ineffective--everything was out of sync and everyone had a voice but no one had a shared view or opinion. For a leadership team to be effective it's absolutely critical to have trust and openness and it requires giving more of yourself. You need to be honest, to be ready to take criticism and be open to having your decisions be questioned by others. You need to offer objective commentary, ask the question, "why?" and be willing to ask the kinds of questions that can enrich your view of your slice of the world.

Not every CRO will start with a company on Day One and be able to grow with the leadership team and more often than not, you may find that you're the newly hired CRO in a new company with a leadership team you know nothing about. While it is obviously the responsibility of the CEO to foster the environment that would enable a new person to contribute to the team immediately, there are practices any leadership team can undertake that will be effective in helping the team perform better. One practice that works really well is to have each person on the leadership team write their bio. Not a typical bio, but one where you write, here's who I am, here's how I think, here's how I work most effectively, here's what I'm very good at, here's where my weaknesses are, here's where I could use her help, here's what I hope to accomplish.

If each person on the leadership team has that bio, they can share it with the others and this promotes an openness and candor that sets the stage for you as a new person on the leadership team and gives people an understanding of how you think, how you work, and how you want to work with them. Similarly, if you have a cohesive team and you're welcoming the new member, beyond sharing your bios, it's equally important to let them know what works for this team, what's been really successful and what hasn't.

As a CRO you will likely have strong interdependencies with a few other parts of the business, like marketing and product and it's important to be able to connect with the leaders of those functions and try to form a shared vision. For example, earlier in my career as a revenue leader, when I would walk into the engineering room everyone would scatter, they would run for the hills. I assumed that the mindset of engineers was that they don't care as much about revenue as they care about what feature they just created that really jazzed customers. As the CRO I would only talk about revenue, how we were doing, what the pipeline was like, where we're seeing an uptick in orders—that kind of thing. And I found that there was a disconnect, that my focus on revenues wasn't resonating with the engineering team.

What I learned to do instead was to orient myself around other people's perspectives and I became very deliberate about being sure that I had one-on-one connection with every head on the leadership team--product, marketing, engineering, HR, and finance so that we could understand one another's perspectives. With that shared understanding it was more likely that the head of engineering, for example, would introduce me to his engineering leaders and we could talk about why the customer wants certain features in products. Our conversations became much more productive because now the engineering team is not creating products for the sake of creating products, but creating for a purpose.

It's really important to have those one-on-one relationships with each member of the executive team and that will ideally help you, as a new CRO, to forge relationships throughout the organization and all layers of management.

21

Fractional Chief Revenue Officer

B.J. Bushur

I've always been in B2B sales and in technology companies. I started my career as a sales rep at a company that got bought by PricewaterhouseCoopers where I learned both sales and management skills. I got the amazing opportunity to go to Netscape right when the first browser was launched in 1994. Netscape didn't have sales reps, just tech support, so I went there as the first sales rep starting as inside sales and then took over the inside sales organization. And over the five and a half years I was there, I got to see how the rocket ship took off when we went public. By then we were selling enterprise solutions and I ran a 100-person inside sales organization with quota bearing reps, sales development reps, and account managers who would renew and upsell customers.

After we were bought by AOL, I decided it was time to follow Marc Andreessen and Ben Horowitz over to what was then called Loudcloud. We were a managed services organization (in 2000) selling the whole web operation, people, and technology stack to SasS companies. That's when I really learned lots of the ins and outs of changing the go-to-market models, when I'd had my first baby, and when I decided I loved working with startups. Ever since then I've been working with B2B technology companies to set up or strengthen their sales foundation for scale. I work with them to surround their sales organization with the processes, tools, systems, compensation, enablement, and metrics to scale a fast growth startup.

Becoming a Fractional Executive

Becoming a fractional executive is part skills and part mindset. By that I mean, one of the things that holds talented, credible, impactful people back from taking on a fractional role is the fear of the unknown. Can I do this? Will I make enough money? How do I get clients? Will the work be steady or will I constantly be searching for new opportunities? There are a lot of big unknowns in the beginning and those fears can prevent you from doing something you love. What helped me to overcome these fears and doubts was working with a leadership coach to peel back those unknowns. Could my family afford it? Could I get enough business? What would the barriers be? How difficult would it be to work with different companies? The coach I worked with helped me uncover those unknowns and I researched them so I could make that informed decision on whether a fractional role would work or not.

I also worked with a financial planner because so much of the risk that you take is actually not about being capable of doing the work, but about whether or not you can survive financially. Working with a financial planner really helped me and my family figure out if it was feasible. We had to understand our health insurance options because we were both self-employed. We had to figure out our childcare situation and costs. So, a first step was just researching the unknowns and asking, can we live with that? Because your income looks variable at first, when you're a fractional leader, I had to know if I would be able to weather those unknowns and I had to trust that even if the worst-case scenario happens, I could live with that.

The other thing that's important to know, if you're thinking about the fractional role, is what you're good at and what you love. They're not always the same. I needed to understand, what are the things I enjoy doing and I'm good at? What are the necessary evils of running sales that maybe I'm not good at, or bore me, or frustrate me? For me, it was systems. I knew how to use Salesforce .com (back then it was a newer technology) and I was good at it. But it bores me. I didn't want to get deep into the technology and I'd much rather work on solution selling, coaching sales reps on deals, hiring great talent, and enabling sales reps. So, my first year was a lot of experimenting on what are the projects and the situations at the client that excite me, energize me, that I'm good at, and that I *want* to do, versus going down the rabbit hole of things I don't really enjoy doing.

One situation really drove this point home for me. A client hired me just to recruit their inside sales function which I happily accepted because I thought I would have a lot of interaction with the sales management team. But I was siloed off just with HR and never really engaged with the sales side of the house; I just helped screen candidates. And I realized when I was pigeonholed into a small piece of sales management that it frustrated me; I wanted a bigger picture, I wanted to be working hand-in-hand with the sales leader and help with bigger strategy. I learned to say "no" to those things and now I partner with people who are really good at those other things. Surrounding yourself with the rest of what needs to be successful for your C-function is a key to being successful as a fractional executive.

Finding Fractional Roles

Once you're established, it's relatively easy to find fractional roles. All of my work comes through referrals, from past clients in my network, from clients or CEOs who have moved, and from VCs primarily. But what about starting out? Before Bolster, there wasn't really a network that brought together companies and fractional executives so you had to leverage your own network. I started by conducting free webinars and (before COVID) I'd do in-person breakfasts or lunches on a topic that's really important to CEOs. I did seminars on common misconceptions about high velocity selling or sales and marketing collaboration—topics that I knew a lot about and that some CEOs would be interested in. That's one way to do it.

Another way to get traction when you're starting out is to network with the most networked people in your network. For example, I had two bosses who retired and one of them really retired and didn't network while the other one was out there with VCs networking all the time and connecting people with great talent/portfolio's needs. So, I spent a lot of time with the second one, not the first one. So, figure out who those people are who are networking and make sure they know and trust you so that you can meet the people who will want to hire you.

Cautionary Advice

One thing I learned very early on in doing this is to trust your gut because when you start out, you're in a new situation with a lot of unknowns and you don't know the lay of the land; you haven't figured out yet what could be a problem. During my first year as a fractional executive, I got introduced to some teams where they wanted me to change their go-to-market strategy. I got a call from one leader who asked if I could listen in on a strategy session with the whole C-level team. I responded with, what would be your goal of my participation? The executive countered with, just come for half the day, not the whole day. My gut reaction and what I asked was, why would I want to do that? Why do you need me there? And what would be the outcome of that? The executive couldn't tell me.

I called my former boss whom I trusted, immensely, and who was a very good friend of mine as well as one of my mentors and heroes. I told him that I'm new to this whole fractional thing and should I be expected to just go for a half day not understanding what's going on? He said, "No, there's some management dysfunction there." But then I questioned myself. Should I have just gone? I didn't have anything else going on. It ended up not panning out and the company was dysfunctional. So just because you're new to being a fractional leader, still trust your gut and if a company can't articulate exactly why they need you and what they want you to be doing for them, it's probably not going to work out. If I'm in that situation now, if I realize that it's not a cultural fit or they know they need help but can't pin it down, I just say I'm too busy to take on the role.

When a company can't describe the deliverables that they want, or what skills they need from you, or what outcomes they want to happen—if they can't describe those, then they're probably not ready for any fractional executive. If a company wants a bunch of free strategy sessions, then trust your gut that if they're not willing to pay for even some small assessment that's probably an indication that they're not valuing your skill set or they don't know what they need enough. Getting a sense of what are the macro goals that they're trying to hit, understanding their current challenges, and making sure that your skill set, your experience, and what you want to do are a match for you in that situation are the keys to being a successful fractional executive.

One other important thing for a CRO: you definitely need to understand whether the company you'll be working with has product market fit because if they don't have product market fit for whatever they're asking you to sell, you won't be able to make an impact. I had a project where the CEO thought they had product market fit, and the CEO was passionate about it. It was a younger CEO, a first-time CEO, a technology CEO and I should have paid more attention to what others were telling me about where they were in their product life cycle instead of taking the CEO's word for it. I'm sure it differs by domain for other C-level roles like Finance or HR, but you need to make sure that you can actually impact the company. You need to make sure that some of the fundamentals are in place, for whatever role you're doing. You may have to triangulate with the other managers to be able to answer the question, what needs to be in place for you to be able to have an impact?

I'm passionate about fractional roles because I think people can have a much better life if they choose this route and they can make a truly impactful contribution to a company. You just have to peel back those unknowns and go for it!

22

Fractional Chief Revenue Officer

Sherri Sklar

One of the things that I like about working in a fractional role is that elements from your entire career can come into play, enabling you to make a large impact in a relatively short period of time. Many emerging tech companies often get to product market fit, only to stall when trying to grow and scale. The talent that got the company to that point may or may not be enough to take the company to the next level. From a revenue perspective, there are timely decisions that need to be made operationally—in your go-to-market strategy and in your execution—that can make or break your next growth cycle. It takes a seasoned senior executive who has lived the various parts of the revenue function under many different previous stress tests, to know which strategy and which move is the least risky and most likely to succeed.

I started selling IBM mainframes right out of college and when I left IBM I was running a $40 million business. When I went to the startup world everything went out the window. In the new world of tech startups, I started at the basement level to learn the business from the bottom up. I began again as a sales rep and from there to district manager, regional manager, VP Sales, and then went over to the marketing side to become a VP Marketing, and finally became a VP of Business Development. Over the course of my career, I had the opportunity to wear every kind of revenue hat in large organizations and in startup organizations. As a fractional executive, that provides a lot of credibility. When I walk in the door, everybody knows that I've been in their shoes at one point or another in my career; it creates instant trust knowing that I have carried a bag, that I know what I'm talking about, and that I can speak as well from a Sales perspective as I can from a Marketing perspective as I can from a Customer Success perspective.

Companies that I work with bring me in to help run their organizations and they typically are a Series A or Series B company who may not have a revenue leader or the right kind of leadership in place. These companies are at a point where they need somebody who understands how to achieve growth and scale. They need a fractional CRO to take the revenue functions off of the CEO's plate so the CEO can focus on other critical actions to help the company grow, such as fundraising, product strategy, development, people, culture, and driving the vision for the company. The fractional CRO can enable the CEO to move forward, confident that the right decisions are also being made on the revenue side of the house.

I love this work so much because I get a chance to implement my twin passions for helping companies to grow and helping companies become customer-centric so they can truly make a difference in their customers' lives. I usually come in right before a CEO realizes they need somebody permanently. So, it's almost like they could try it out with me and then sometimes they realize, "Oh, my gosh, I need somebody full-time." So, my role is to get them structured and set up for really great results and help pave the way for a full-time CRO.

Qualities of a Fractional CRO

One key to being successful as a fractional CRO is to be comfortable in your own skin. You have to believe in yourself and be a great leader in the face of many people who may question your every move, which can happen for a variety of reasons. You might be the only one in the company at this point who knows the best way forward, and you need to remember it's your experience and your know-how that got you here. Believe in yourself and stand up for what you believe in. Help others in your new companies understand the path they must take, even if it's unfamiliar territory to them.

It's also important to know how to be a leader as a fractional because you may not have full authority that everybody who works for you thinks or expects you to have. Many times I have been brought in as the CRO but did not have full authority to price deals, make hiring decisions, or manage certain personnel issues without having the CEO or some other executive approve. Constraints on your authority can be a consequence of nothing other than being in a position of authority but technically not being a full-time employee. Sometimes, unintentionally, that can send the wrong message—that you are not trusted by your CEO. Other times it can be incredibly frustrating to your people, because without having full authority, processes can get longer rather than shorter. One way to counteract this situation is by having a proactive discussion with your CEO upfront before your contract starts. Ask them if there is a way around some of these legal technicalities so that you can gain full authority. If you can't get full authority, maybe you can set processes up that serve to streamline rather than frustrate people.

Another quality that a fractional executive needs is to be comfortable with ambiguity and uncertainty. How long will you be with the company? A lot of times you don't know—it could be 3 months, 6 months, a year, or even longer. Or it could be at some trigger event. I worked with a company to help them in a fundraising round. When they successfully got it, the PE firm that took them over wanted to put their own person in. You have to be comfortable with the fact that you might do a wonderful job, and they may still not want you to stay as the full-time CRO. On the other hand, you also should expect that if you do a wonderful job, you may very well be asked to stay on as the full-time CXO.

What to Expect as a Fractional CRO

You should expect that in a startup or scaleup company that the day you show up you'll be faced with a myriad of issues that have to be addressed. A fractional CRO needs to be aware that there's going to be a ton of processes and urgent situations that need addressing and need fixing. Fractional CROs need to expect that many parts of the organization they are walking into are broken. This is not a "red flag" about whether this situation is a good opportunity for you or not. You're there precisely because many things may be broken and because you are the best at fixing and optimizing. The fractional CRO will relish these challenges—this is how you know you are in the right place at the right time.

If you have to move on, it can be difficult. If you are there for a limited or certain period of time only, it can be hard to move on because you end up loving the people with whom you work—whether it's the senior executive team or the people that work for you. It's just like any kind of job where you get into a new relationship with people and a company—you form relationships, you have achieved a certain set of results, you're proud of your work, and it can be hard to move on from that.

Another challenge about the job is that as a fractional executive, it's often hard because the expectation is to achieve the full result within a fraction of the time. Many times you end up putting in 100–150% of your time, simply because the workload is so hefty, you will feel like you have to address the issues head-on and immediately. Often the issues you are being asked to address can't wait for you to be available during the part-time hours that were pre-arranged. So, you have to be careful to set expectations going in, that in the event that the workload is much higher than anticipated, you can reset expectations and renegotiate your contract based on what has shown itself to be more realistic.

The Good Part

The good part of being a fractional executive is that you get a chance to do what you love and really make a difference to a CEO who really needs you. And that is exciting. You're bringing your expertise that nobody else in the company has, you're helping that CEO and the Board get results that they never could have gotten without you—all in a very compressed amount of time. You get the chance to prove yourself, to make a difference for somebody. And in the fractional world, you can help many companies in this way.

23

CEO-to-CEO Advice About the Sales Role

Matt Blumberg

What comes before a full-fledged CRO? In most startups, the founder is the first salesperson. As startups scale, they add sales reps or maybe some form of a sales manager once there are more than a couple of reps. In the journey Anita writes about—from "selling on whiteboard" to "selling with PowerPoint" to "selling with PDF"—all of this is in the whiteboard stage and beginning to make the transition to PowerPoint.

Signs It's Time to Hire Your First CRO

You know it's time to hire a CRO when:

- You wake up in the middle of the night concerned about HOW you're going to make this quarter's number—not just WHETHER or not you'll make it (since you should know that as much as anyone), but that you aren't clear what the levers are, or what the pipeline/forecast details are, to get there.

- You are spending too much of your own time managing individual deals and pricing, or teaching individual reps how to get jobs done.

- Your Board asks you if you're ready to step on the gas and scale your revenue engine (e.g., move from PowerPoint to PDF), and you don't have a great answer and aren't sure how to get to one.

When a Fractional CRO Might Be Enough

A fractional CRO may be the way to go if:

- Even at small volume where you wouldn't yet be ready for a full-time CRO, your sales operation is very complex or to a very senior buyer, and a more junior sales team needs a fair amount of deal support from above.

- You're entering a new adjacent segment (e.g., mid-market going to enterprise), and you need a seasoned professional to help translate sales process from one segment to the other while keeping the initial segment running smoothly.

- You are not sure what kind of sales leader you need long-term and full-time because you're not at enough scale yet, but you want to try out a specific type of revenue leader to see if that type works (e.g., sales only, sales + customer success, manager of hunters, builder of a high velocity sales engine).

What Does Great Look Like in a CRO?

Ideal startup CROs do five things particularly well:

1. They know when to turn up the volume, and when not to. Thinking through our metaphor/framework for enterprise sales that

Anita writes about in this Part—from whiteboard to PowerPoint to PDF—great CROs know when they aren't yet in PDF mode. In the early days when your organization is selling on whiteboard or figuring out the transition to PowerPoint, adding sales reps like crazy, even if there is a lot of opportunity to pursue, is inefficient and unlikely to be successful because it still depends on the success of individual hunters. Only when the organization has made the true transition to PDF can a sales machine scale rapidly.

2. They give credit to others first when things go well and look inward first when things go poorly. Great CROs are the first ones to thank their fellow executives in Marketing, in Product, in Finance, for collaboration and successes. They are also the first ones to thank their team publicly for a good quarter. When they miss a quarter, the first thing they do is figure out why the Sales team blew it, as opposed to blaming the product or marketing.

3. They are maniacally focused on building a conveyor belt–style pipeline for sales talent so they don't lose momentum when a rep quits or gets fired. "Quota just walked out the door" is never an excuse in a well-tuned sales machine where multiple layers of reps are consistently trained, managed, and groomed for the next level of selling.

4. They say no to over-paying and over-promoting. The second-worst thing a sales leader can do is get compensation wrong by paying reps too much base, or have too much commission in easily-repeatable form. Reps who are over-paid get "fat and happy," when what you want is for them to be "lean and hungry." The worst thing a CRO can do is promote a superstar sales rep with no management aptitude or training into a sales manager role. That will not only lead to the person getting fired, it has the potential to poison a whole sales team. Great CROs know how to say no to the misguided request for a promotion.

5. They don't believe in the "magic rolodex" (yes, I realize that term

is a bit dated!). Unless you are hiring a sales rep who literally just finished selling a competitive solution to the same target customer set, sales reps who claim they come with a built-in book of business can only deliver on that promise 1% of the time. It's alluring—but it just doesn't work out that way. Great CROs know how to ferret that out.

Signs Your CRO Isn't Scaling

CROs who aren't scaling well past the startup stage are the ones who typically:

- Gravitate to being an individual contributor sales rep and focus on closing big deals instead of mentoring sales managers and sales reps to do that work on their own. To be clear, sometimes the role of a sales leader (or a CEO) is to swoop in and help close a big deal. But CROs who can't shake their addiction to closing deals almost never build enough of that muscle into their organization and end up creating an unhealthy dependency on them.

- Get sales commission plans out in March or April. While it's true that, in a lot of businesses, it's very difficult to get sales commission plans out until after the year starts, getting them out after late February is a sign that your CRO doesn't have enough of a grip on numbers, isn't partnering effectively with Finance, doesn't care enough about their people, or isn't good at prioritizing the important over the urgent when needed. "They'll all be fine, they know I'll take care of them, the plan is a lot like last year's" isn't good enough for the best reps who are constantly doing sales math in their heads.

- Regularly deliver surprises at the end of the quarter—both good and bad surprises. This is a sign of a scaling problem—either your CRO doesn't have a good grip on the pipeline and in particular on larger deals; they are bad at managing expectations; or both!

How I Engage with the CRO

A few ways I've typically spent the most time or gotten the most value out of CROs over the years are:

- During travel time or in and around events. Particularly if you're a B2B company that engages with clients during the sales process, you'll probably find yourself at a lot of client meetings and events, either internal or external. Your CRO will be there, too, which gives you a great opportunity to spend large blocks of time together in transit. One thing we're learning during the work-at-home pandemic is just how much time we save by not traveling. So, when life resumes to normal, why waste time in an Uber or on a plane when you can have a deep strategic con-versation or even a personal/social one with one of your senior executives? Because that early morning time in the hotel gym or late night drink in the lobby bar before heading up to bed could be the time you have a breakthrough with some tricky client-facing issue.

- In a Weekly Forecast meeting. Jeff Epstein, former CFO of Oracle, was one of my long-time Board members at Return Path, and helped us architect a new core business process once our sales team got large and mature and geographically disparate enough that it was hard for us to have a solid forecast. By our CFO and me personally engaging in a Weekly Forecast meeting every week, we forced the discipline of a good roll-up of all regions and business units, and the CRO and all sales managers attended and knew that we were paying attention to the numbers and trends and asking tough questions. The result was that our CRO did a pre-meeting the prior day with all teams and units to prepare, and that in and of itself had a cascading effect through the organization of adding discipline, rigor, and accuracy to the forecast. It also made me a lot more empathetic to my CRO's issues with respect to the sales leadership team.

- Ad hoc, either internally or in-market. My most successful Heads of Sales have been good at winding me up and pointing me at things as needed, whether that means getting on a plane or Zoom to help close a deal or save a client, or doing a one-to-one mentoring session with a key employee.

24

Conclusion

In Sales, nothing is ever "in the bag." I cringe when I hear an overly optimistic salesperson display that level of bravado and confidence in the absence of actual data. A "good feeling" does not equate to success. And I often tell a salesperson that I don't care about their feelings, I care about the facts (in the most supportive way, of course). Another saying here, that may or not be appropriate, is that "it ain't over till the fat lady sings." When I joined Return Path, the original, departing VP Sales, who was a friend and colleague, assured me that $6m was "in the bag," for the year, although we only had just over $3m in sales at the time. I believed him, because I thought he had great "gut" instincts, and it was part of the reason I joined Return Path ... although certainly not the primary one. Needless to say, the cumulative sales for that particular product line (which we later sold) never totaled $6m after several years. Lesson learned. "In the bag" became a funny euphemism for something that might never actually happen.

Although the particulars of your own Chief Revenue Officer role will differ from mine, and while you'll undoubtedly have a very different career path than me, I can say with complete confidence that if you want to build a great sales organization, the approaches I outline in this book will certainly get you there. If you're fortunate in your career you'll get to work with extraordinary people, totally aligned to turn your startup into a thriving enterprise—but it's not necessary. If you understand the importance of having scalable and repeatable processes, of working with direct and channel sales teams, of looking carefully at efficiency and productivity metrics, and of managing a business to the bottom line, you'll be able to make a big difference in your company. And the sales organization will pull the rest of the company forward.

The easiest, fastest, and most gratifying way to build a great sales organization is to cultivate a culture that's people-focused, one that provides opportunities for coaching, mentorship, and career growth for your employees and, yes, one where successful salespeople are amply and properly recognized and rewarded financially. If you work with and through others to execute on the vision, engage teams in the vision, collaborate for success, hold each other to high standards of performance and accountability, you'll have the foundation for building a great organization.

So, let me end with a few thoughts on what "great" looks like.

- Great is running an organization with a common sense of purpose, shared commitment, and enthusiasm.

- Great is creating a team culture of learning, sharing, and mentoring others.

- Great is representing a product or solution you believe in, and helping your prospects and customers solve business problems.

- Great is providing an environment where people can be successful, and advance in their careers.

- Great is being part of an organization that collaborates for success and holds itself and its people to high standards of performance and accountability.

- Great is being easy to work with, internally and externally.

Acknowledgements

This book is derivative of *Startup CXO* and the acknowledgments for this book extends to the people who helped in that effort. The list of people to thank for their role in helping create that is long and has to start with my current and former colleagues who were the primary contributors: Jack Sinclair, Cathy Hawley, Shawn Nussbaum, Ken Takahashi, Nick Badgett, Holly Enneking, Anita Absey, George Bilbrey, Dennis Dayman, and Dave Wilby. *Startup CXO* was a truly collaborative work and the same is true with this book. Anita and I collaborated together and also with Pete Birkeland, who edited the second edition of *Startup CEO*, was a tireless collaborator for *Startup CXO*, and helped bring this book to fruition.

I would also like to acknowledge the rest of the Bolster team and board that made this possible, especially this book's project manager, Rachel Henry. It wasn't easy to carve out the time to write while scaling up Bolster, much less doing the bulk of the writing over the holidays and I'm grateful to all the contributors for their effort.

Although the professional lives of the contributors are now primarily at Bolster, most of us worked together for many years at Return Path, and all of us would like to thank our Board and shareholders, particularly Fred Wilson, Greg Sands, Scott Weiss, Scott Petry, Jeff Epstein, and Brad Feld (more on Brad in a minute) for giving us the opportunity to learn on the job as we scaled ourselves and scaled the business over the better part of two decades. That experience is what led us to be able to write *Startup CXO*. We'd also like to thank all 1,300 colleagues from Return Path over the years who challenged, inspired, and taught us things every day. Although he was not a Return Path or Bolster team member, Marc Maltz from Hoola Hoop Consulting, my long-time partner as an executive coach, has shaped the thinking of me and of a number of the contributors to this effort.

Startup CXO is part of the *Startup Revolution* series that was created by my long-time board member and friend Brad Feld. Brad's advice on all things business, personal, and writing has been invaluable for over 20 years and whether attributed or not, many of the ideas in this book are the result of many thoughtful conversations with him. I would also like to thank the team at Wiley (Bill Falloon and Purvi Patel) for their help and support as editors, publishers, and marketers.

Startup CXO had a very large number of people who contributed their insights to the final form, which carries over to this book, including sidebars by Rob Krolik and Jeff Epstein, Guy Turner, Greg Sands, Scott Petry, Brad Feld, Dave Wilby, and Scott Dorsey. We are also grateful for the contribution to our fractional chapters from B.J. Bushur and Sherri Sklar.

We received a number of thoughtful comments on specific functional areas from Rick Buck, Caroline Pearl, Diana Caleroni, Jen Goldman, Mike Mutone, Debby Meredith, and Chad Shinsato. Brad Feld and Scott Dorsey did a final read-through of the entire book (not a small feat!) and provided helpful suggestions to the final work.

I want to end by thanking my family for their unwavering support as I embarked on a series of books while scaling a second startup—a combination that I can't exactly endorse as being sane or smart. *Startup CXO* was a collaborative effort but I would have been the anchor holding us back if it weren't for my wife of over two decades, Mariquita. My thanks start and end with her. An executive coach for startup CEOs, Mariquita has been intimately involved in all my professional projects, providing advice, encouragement, and support to whatever I'm doing.

Matt Blumberg

About the Authors

Matt Blumberg. Matt has spent his entire career creating startups, scaling them, and sharing best practices of what works and what doesn't work for other CEOs and team members in the entrepreneurial community. He is the author of *Startup CEO: A Field Guide to Scaling Up Your Business* (Wiley, 2020), an influential book embraced by entrepreneurs, CEOs, founders, and board of directors in the entrepreneurial ecosystem. Startup CEO was an outgrowth of his blog, StartupCEO.com. In 1999, he founded Return Path, an innovative email marketing company, helped it to $100m in revenues, and led it to a successful exit in a strategic sale to Validity in 2019. Along with colleagues from Return Path, Matt started Bolster in 2020, a company focused on helping startups and scaleups grow, develop, and scale their leadership teams and boards. Matt's second book, *Startup CXO: A Field Guide to Scaling Up Your Company's Critical Functions and Teams* (Wiley, 2021), was a collaboration with Bolster's CXOs to provide a blueprint for scaling up each function.

Before Return Path, Matt led Marketing, Product Management, and the Internet Group for MovieFone, Inc. (later acquired by AOL). Prior to that, he served as an associate with private equity firm General Atlantic Partners and was a consultant with Mercer Management Consulting. He also cofounded and chairs the board of Path Forward, a nonprofit created and spun out of Return Path. Path Forward's mission is to empower people to restart their careers after time spent focused on caregiving by working with companies offering mid-career internships. Path Forward gives women and men a path to a professional career, while giving companies access to a diverse, untapped talent force. Matt is currently Executive Chair at Bolster. He earned his A.B. from Princeton University.

Anita Absey. Anita began her career on Wall Street in equity research, risk arbitrage, and corporate finance, but for the past 20 years has had wide-ranging roles in sales. Anita has been in sales leadership positions in startups and scaleups including Abacus Direct, DoubleClick, Return Path, and Voxy. Anita views her success through the lens of revenue growth and customer satisfaction and her greatest satisfaction comes from watching people on her teams thrive in their careers. Anita contributed to *Startup CXO: A Field Guide to Scaling Up Your Company's Critical Functions and Teams* (Wiley, 2021), sharing her experience, tips, and best practices for CROs to build a great sales organization. She earned a BA in economics at Fordham University.